بسم الله الرحمن الرحيم

ABOUT THE AUTHOR

The author, who writes under the pen-name HARUN YAHYA, was born in Ankara in 1956. Having completed his primary and secondary education in Ankara, he then studied arts at Istanbul's Mimar Sinan University and philosophy at Istanbul University. Since the 1980s, the author has published many books on political, faith-related and scientific issues. Harun Yahya is well-known as an author who has written very important works disclosing the imposture of evolutionists, the invalidity of their claims and the dark liaisons between Darwinism and bloody ideologies.

His pen-name is made up of the names "Harun" (Aaron) and "Yahya" (John), in memory of the two esteemed prophets who fought against lack of faith. The Prophet's seal on the cover of the author's books has a symbolic meaning linked to the their contents. This seal represents the Koran as the last Book by Allah and the last word of Him and our Prophet, the last of all the prophets. Under the guidance of the Koran and Sunnah, the author makes it his main goal to disprove each one of the fundamental tenets of godless ideologies and to have the "last word", so as to completely silence the objections raised against religion. The seal of the Prophet, who attained ultimate wisdom and moral perfection, is used as a sign of his intention of saying this last word.

All these works by the author centre around one goal: to convey the message of the Koran to people, thus encouraging them to think about basic faith-related issues, such as the existence of Allah, His unity and the hereafter, and to display the decrepit foundations and perverted works of godless systems.

Harun Yahya enjoys a wide readership in many countries, from India to America, England to Indonesia, Poland to Bosnia, and Spain to Brazil. Some of his books are available in English, French, German, Italian, Portuguese, Urdu, Arabic, Albanian, Russian, Serbo-Croat (Bosnian), Uygur Turkish, and Indonesian, and they have been enjoyed by readers all over the world.

Greatly appreciated all around the world, these works have been instrumental in many people putting their faith in Allah and in many others gaining a deeper insight into their faith. The wisdom, and the sincere and easy-to-understand style employed give these books a distinct touch which directly strikes any one who reads or examines them. Immune to objections, these works are characterised by their features of rapid effectiveness, definite results and irrefutability. It is unlikely that those who read these books and give a serious thought to them can any longer sincerely advocate the materialistic philosophy, atheism and any other perverted ideology or philosophy. Even if they continue to advocate, this will be only a sentimental insistence since these books have refuted these ideologies from their very basis. All contemporary movements of denial are ideologically defeated today, thanks to the collection of books written by Harun Yahya.

There is no doubt that these features result from the wisdom and lucidity of the Koran. The author certainly does not feel proud of himself; he merely intends to serve as a means in one's search for Allah's right path. Furthermore, no material gain is sought in the publication of these works.

Considering these facts, those who encourage people to read these books, which open the "eyes" of the heart and guide them in becoming more devoted servants of Allah, render an invaluable service.

Meanwhile, it would just be a waste of time and energy to propagate books which create confusion in peoples' minds, lead man into ideological chaos, and which, clearly have no strong and precise effects in removing the doubts in peoples' hearts, as also verified from previous experience. It is apparent that it is impossible for books devised to emphasize the author's literary power rather than the noble goal of saving people from loss of faith, to have such a great effect. Those who doubt this can readily see that the sole aim of Harun Yahya's books is to overcome disbelief and to disseminate the moral values of the Koran. The success, impact and sincerity this service has attained are manifest in the reader's conviction.

One point needs to be kept in mind: The main reason for the continuing cruelty and conflict, and all the ordeals Muslims undergo is the ideological prevalence of disbelief. These things can only come to an end with the ideological defeat of disbelief and by ensuring that everybody knows about the wonders of creation and Koranic morality, so that people can live by it. Considering the state of the world today, which forces people into the downward spiral of violence, corruption and conflict, it is clear that this service has to be provided more speedily and effectively. Otherwise, it may be too late.

It is no exaggeration to say that the collection of books by Harun Yahya have assumed this leading role. By the Will of Allah, these books will be the means through which people in the 21st century will attain the peace and bliss, justice and happiness promised in the Koran.

WONDERS OF ALLAH'S CREATION

To The Reader

In all the books by the author, faith-related issues are explained in the light of the Koranic verses and people are invited to learn Allah's words and to live by them. All the subjects that concern Allah's verses are explained in such a way as to leave no room for doubt or question marks in the reader's mind. The sincere, plain and fluent style employed ensures that everyone of every age and from every social group can easily understand the books. This effective and lucid narrative makes it possible to read them in a single sitting. Even those who rigorously reject spirituality are influenced by the facts recounted in these books and cannot refute the truthfulness of their contents.

This book and all the other works of the author can be read individually or discussed in a group at a time of conversation. Those readers who are willing to profit from the books will find discussion very useful in the sense that they will be able to relate their own reflections and experiences to one another.

In addition, it will be a great service to the religion to contribute to the presentation and reading of these books, which are written solely for the good pleasure of Allah. All the books of the author are extremely convincing. For this reason, for those who want to communicate the religion to other people, one of the most effective methods is to encourage them to read these books.

It is hoped that the reader will take time to look through the review of other books on the final pages of the book, and appreciate the rich source of material on faith-related issues, which are very useful and a pleasure to read.

In these books, you will not find, as in some other books, the personal views of the author, explanations based on dubious sources, styles that are unobservant of the respect and reverence due to sacred subjects, nor hopeless, doubt-creating, and pessimistic accounts that create deviations in the heart.

WONDERS OF ALLAH'S CREATION

HARUN YAHYA

Ta-Ha Publishers Ltd.
I Wynne Road London SW9 OBB
United Kingdom

May, 2004

All translations from the Qur'an are from
"The Noble Qur'an: a New Rendering of its Meaning in English"
by Hajj Abdalhaqq and Aisha Bewley,
published by Bookwork, Norwich, UK. 1420 CE/1999 AH

By Harun Yahya

Translated By: Tuba Addas
Edited By: Abdassamad Clarke

A catalog record of this book is available from the British Library
ISBN 1-84200-037-3

Printed and bound by:
Secil Ofset in Istanbul
100 Yıl Mahallesi MAS-SIT Matbaacilar Sitesi 4. Cadde No: 77
Bagcilar-Istanbul / TURKEY Phone: (+90) 212 629 06 15

Website: www.harunyahya.com
E-mail: info@harunyahya.com

CONTENTS

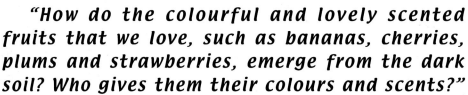

INTRODUCTION

Children!

Did you ever wonder?

"How did the universe form?"

"How did the sun and the moon begin to exist?"

"Where were you before you were born?"

"How did the seas, trees, and animals come about?"

"How do the colourful and lovely scented fruits that we love, such as bananas, cherries, plums and strawberries, emerge from the dark soil? Who gives them their colours and scents?"

"From where does the tiny bee learn how to make such tasty honey? How does he make a honeycomb that has such smooth corners?"

"Who was the first human?"

"Your mother gave birth to you. But the first human couldn't have had a mother or a father. So how did the first human all of a sudden appear?"

In this book, you will learn the correct answer to all of these questions.

Do you know what this correct answer is? Everything that you see around you, including

yourself, your friends, your parents, the earth, the sun, the food that you love, bananas, cherries, strawberries, colourful roses, violets, beautiful scents, human beings, cats, dogs, ants, bees, horses, birds and butterflies, in short everything was created by Allah.

We asked you, "Did you ever think: from where does the tiny bee learn how to make such tasty honey?" Well, Allah is the One Who teaches the bee how to make honey.

But there are those people who tell stories about these things. They don't believe that Allah has created everything and they invent stories about it. These people are called "evolutionists" and the story that they tell is called "evolution".

We want you to learn what is the truth, and that is why we have started by telling you the right things. In the second part of the book, we will show you how those who believe in evolution deceive people. If after you have read this book, someone comes up to you one day and asks you to believe in the theory of evolution, you can then tell him that the theory of evolution is not right, and Allah is the Creator of everything.

HOW DID THE

Do you know what the universe is? It is endless space and everything that it holds, earth, the sun, the moon, the planets and the stars. Even if you walk millions and millions of miles you will not be able to reach the end of space, and in fact, you have hardly reached its beginning. The reason for that is that space is too large to describe.

Earth exists within this limitless space. Along with earth, the sun, moon, and millions of stars exist in

EARTH

UNIVERSE FORM?

it as well.

So how did all of these things form? How did the sun come into being, for example? Or how did our earth appear?

There are two types of responses to this question. One of these responses is right and the other is wrong. Those who respond wrongly are also believers in the theory of evolution. On the next page, we will first show you the wrong response and then the right one.

MOON

SUN

THE WRONG RESPONSE:

Those who respond incorrectly say: The universe was always there and it came about by itself. That is, a lot of substances came together on their own by chance to form the sun, stars, earth, seas, trees, rivers and mountains.

Don't you think this thought is illogical? If a friend of yours came to you and said something like: "I had put some soil, stones, and a little bit of water inside a big box. I waited for a couple of years and then a computer emerged from this box." Would you believe him? You would probably think that your friend was joking, lying or mad.

Evolutionists openly tell a tall story just like that. A computer cannot form all by itself as a result of some coincidences. First, someone plans what the computer is supposed to be like, and decides what components are to be used. Then, in large factories, engineers, technicians and hundreds of workers come together. They use huge machinery to put the computer together. That is to say, when you see a computer you would know that it did not just happen all by itself. Isn't it obvious that intelligent people make computers?

The sun, earth and other plants are much larger than a computer. So, if there are those who make computers, there must be a power that creates the sun, earth, moon and stars.

THE RIGHT RESPONSE:

Did you understand what the right response is? Allah is the Creator of the sun, earth, planets, and stars. Everything in the universe is perfect and orderly. That is because Allah created the universe, and He has put everything where it belongs.

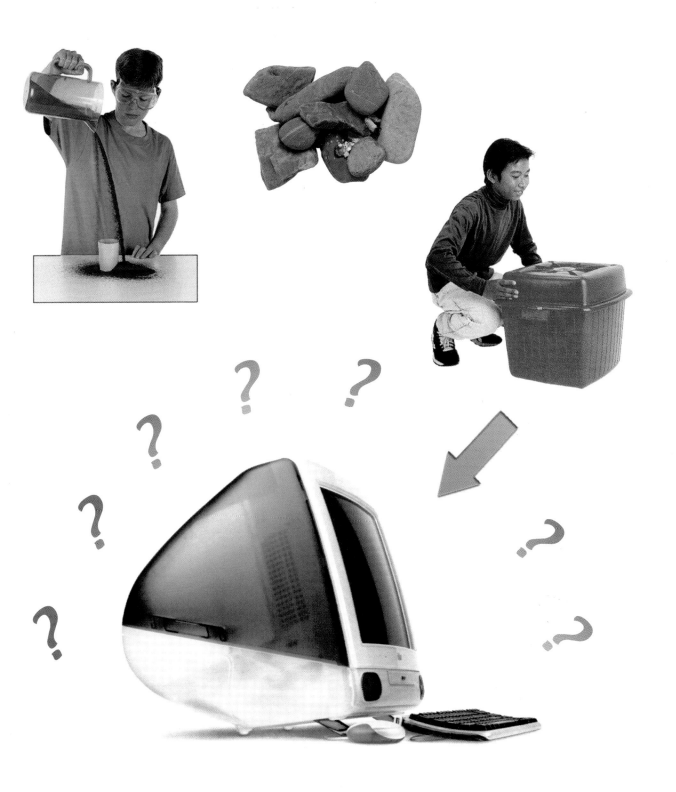

If a friend of yours had put some soil, stones and a little bit of water inside a box and then came to you and said that after waiting for a couple of years a computer emerged from the box, would you not break into laughter at the thought?

HOW DID ALLAH CREATE THE UNIVERSE?

Scientists have made a very important discovery in recent years. This important discovery was that before the universe was formed, there was nothing else. There was no land, no air, no water, and there were no stars; there was even no space. Inside this nothingness, there was this tiny spot. This spot was so tiny that it was difficult even for an eye to see. A lot of matter had been squeezed together inside this spot. Then, in an instant this spot exploded. When it exploded, all the matter that was squeezed inside it flew about. After that, the pieces of matter joined together to first form atoms, then from those atoms, stars, our sun, earth and the other planets. The scientists named this explosion the "Big Bang". Everything in the universe was formed as a result of this Big Bang.

Here you have to think about something very important. Let's imagine that you put the pieces of a puzzle randomly inside a balloon.

After that, you fill your balloon with air and then suddenly pop it. That is to say the balloon "big banged". What happens to the puzzle's pieces that you had stuffed inside the balloon? Could these pieces form a beautiful villa or an airport—something even you could hardly manage—in the middle of your room? Or would they scatter all over the room? Of course, they would scatter all over your room. You would have to put together the puzzle's pieces for them to form an airport or a house.

Allah is the Maker of the "Big Bang", the Organiser of the matter that scattered in space after the "Big Bang". By bringing together all this matter, He is also the Creator of the sun, earth, planets and stars. When Allah wishes something to be, He gives the order "Be" and it comes into being. Allah is Superior and He is the Strongest. His strength is enough for everything. When He wants something, He can create it immediately.

Allah has sent us His book "The Qur'an" through which He introduces Himself and His creation to us. We can find all the right answers to every question from the Qur'an and the Sunnah (The Prophet Muhammad's way of life). For example, when we ask, "How has Allah created everything?" Allah responds in the Qur'an by saying:

"He (Allah) is the Originator of the heavens and the earth... He created all things and He has knowledge of all things." (Surat al-An'am: 101)

ALLAH CREATED EARTH FOR US

Allah is the One Who created earth, the sun, stars and moon. So how did all the living things on earth come into being? Imagine a huge planet with its surface completely empty. There are no humans or animals, no plants or insects.

Earth has been decorated in a lot of detail for living things to survive. Allah is the One Who has given earth all these details. Otherwise none of us would have been able to live, neither you, nor your parents, or indeed any of your friends would have been here.

Let's consider how Allah created the earth so that living things can survive:

1. Think about... how orderly everything in the universe is. The sun has been put in the exact position from which it could warm us and give us light at the same time. If there were no sun, there would not have been one living thing on earth. Neither us, nor the animals nor any other creatures would have been able to live.

2. Allah has also distanced the sun from earth to just the right extent. If earth was a little bit closer to the sun, the heat would have scorched it and we would not have been able to live. If earth was a little more distant from the sun, then glaciers would have covered it and again, few living things would have been able to survive. This is one of the reasons why there is no life on other planets, because they are either too close to the sun or too distant from it.

3. As you know, living things need to breathe in order to live. We need oxygen in the air so that we can breathe. Exactly the right amount of oxygen exists in the air so that human beings can breathe. If there were a little bit more or a little bit less, neither we, nor the animals, nor the plants would have survived,

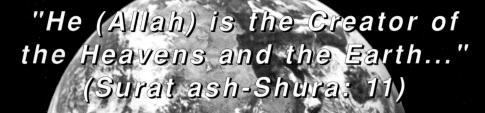

"He (Allah) is the Creator of the Heavens and the Earth..."
(Surat ash-Shura: 11)

because, as we have already said, we need to breathe in order to live. For this we need oxygen.

4. One of the most important things that make it possible for us to survive is water. No organism can live without water. For this reason, Allah has created some parts of earth as water. Three quarters of earth's surface is covered with water. However, there is no water on any of the other planets nor is there any water on the moon that you see at night. The essentials for living things are only available on earth.

Many events on earth make it possible for us to live. If even only one of these events doesn't take place, no living thing would be left on earth. So, is it possible that these thousands of events have come together spontaneously and formed such a place as earth? Of course not. Not even one of these events could happen by chance. Allah has created earth for human beings. And, because of this, earth is the most suitable place for us.

You can give the following example to those that claim earth and the whole universe were formed by chance. Let's say that you are playing on the beach and you see some big waves approaching, so you go home. When you return to the beach after a few hours, you see an amazing sight. On the shore there is a wonderful city made of sand. There are houses, hospitals, an airport, and buses. There are even human figures. You ask a friend who is passing if he knows how these things occurred. If he replied, " I think the big waves that reached the shore must have formed them," what would you think? Wouldn't you be suspicious that your friend imagined it, or wouldn't you laugh thinking that he must be joking or had perhaps become insane?

DO YOU THINK THIS IS POSSIBLE?

You are playing on the beach and, all of a sudden, big waves approach. So, you quickly leave for home.

When you return to the beach after a few hours, you see an amazing sight. There on the shore is a wonderful sandcastle. The recent big waves couldn't have formed this castle "by chance". It is impossible for such a beautiful neat building to have formed by chance, and just in the same way it is impossible for living things to have formed on earth by chance.

IMPOSSIBLE!

It is impossible for waves to have formed such a perfect city from sand by coincidence. It is obvious that someone who is an expert in building such cities had arrived, built it and left.

However, certain people - even though they are professors or scientists - accept such a ridiculous idea. They won't say, "Waves formed the city made of sand", but they would say "Tiny pieces of matter, namely the atoms, came together by chance and they formed the sun, stars and earth all by themselves." This is because these people wouldn't want to say that Allah created everything. They defend the wrong without believing in the right. We will explain who these people are in more detail towards the end of the book.

The Surrounding Protective Shield of Earth: The Atmosphere

Do you know that every day many meteors fall on earth?

Meteors are stones that break off from planets or are the remnants of material from stars. They go about in space, and from time to time fall on the surfaces of planets causing them great damage. But, because Allah has surrounded our planet with a protective shield, they don't do us much harm.

When meteors fall on other planets, they create giant craters, but when they fall on earth, they don't cause much harm.

So how do meteors cause great damage to the surfaces of other planets but not to the surface of earth?

The reason for this is the atmosphere that surrounds earth. The atmosphere encircles our planet as a protective shield. A meteor entering the atmosphere shrinks through combustion. When it comes closer to the surface of earth, it becomes even smaller. Therefore, the meteor becomes very small or even diminishes and disappears completely by the time it reaches the surface of the earth, and causes us no harm.

The atmosphere doesn't only prevent the harm of meteors but it also absorbs harmful rays that come from the Sun. Yet again, if these harmful rays were able to reach earth's surface, it would have been impossible for living things to survive.

The two characteristics we have mentioned here are more than enough to show us that the atmosphere is not some haphazard thing. Allah—Who has endless mercy upon all living things on earth and Who at the same time has eternal power—has created the atmosphere, and with this atmosphere, He protects us from danger.

The atmosphere encircles earth as a protective shield. Thanks to the atmosphere, we are protected from many threats without even realising it.

Can Atoms Think?

As we explained earlier, after the Big Bang, particles emerged and came together as ATOMS. Well, do you know what an atom is?

Let us first explain to you what an atom is like. We can compare the atoms to marbles. But these marbles would be too tiny, unlike anything you have seen before.

Now, look around you! Everything that you see in reality is made of these marbles, namely the atoms. The chair on which you are sitting, the book in your hand, your mother, your teacher at school, the television that you watch, apples, melons, and the chocolates in the kitchen, your pet, water, the flowers in your garden, your toys, and even your body, all are made up of these atoms. As we explained earlier, the stars and suns that make up the universe and the world in which we live are also formed of atoms just like you. In all the places in which you go about and all the corners that you turn, there are atoms.

You cannot see these little things that we call atoms, because they are a lot smaller than you can imagine. They are so small that even with the largest microscopes, it isn't possible to see even one of them. To be able to comprehend the tiny size of the atom, look at this example:

Imagine that you have a key in your hand. Without a doubt, it is impossible for you to see the

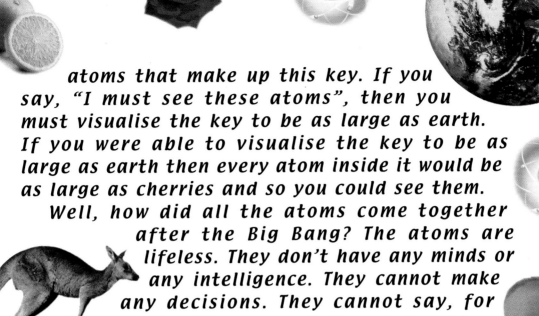

atoms that make up this key. If you say, "I must see these atoms", then you must visualise the key to be as large as earth. If you were able to visualise the key to be as large as earth then every atom inside it would be as large as cherries and so you could see them.

Well, how did all the atoms come together after the Big Bang? The atoms are lifeless. They don't have any minds or any intelligence. They cannot make any decisions. They cannot say, for example, "Come on, let's get together and form a star" or "Let's come closer and form earth". We can also use the following example: We already mentioned a jigsaw puzzle. The pieces of this puzzle are lifeless and, like atoms, they cannot make decisions. If you spread them about, they cannot have thoughts such as "Well, let's get together and form a castle or a human!"

Then let's ask again: "How did all these stars, planets, humans and animals that are made up of atoms come into being? If the atoms did not make a decision, then who put them together?"

Of course, nothing around us can occur by coincidence. Allah is the One Who brings atoms together. Allah has created all the vastness of space, the planets, stars, earth, animals, plants and humans from atoms.

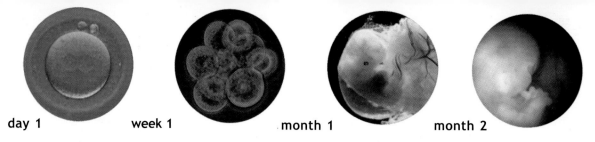

day 1   week 1   month 1   month 2

How are Humans Made of Atoms?

We have said that atoms come together to form human beings, but, of course, you must be wondering how this can happen. First, atoms come together to form CELLS. Again, we are learning something new: So, what is a cell?

The bodies of all living organisms are made up of cells. Even if cells are not as small as atoms, they are still very small and cannot be seen with the naked eye. We can try to explain their tiny size with the following example: If we brought together about 10,000 cells, we could make up something just about the size of the head of a pin. This is why you cannot see them. But cells are the building blocks of humans, ants, cats, roses, trees, and all other living organisms around you. You, for instance, are made up of trillions of cells.

So, where did all these trillions of cells come from?

Look at your brother. He wasn't there two years ago, then all of a sudden he appeared and slowly he started to grow. How did this amazing event happen?

Your brother started out as a single cell in your mother's abdomen. But this single cell was storing a lot of important information inside. All the information that has made your brother into who he is used to be stored in this cell: his eye colour, hair colour, height, etc.

Then this cell grew a little and started to divide. First, it divided in two. However, here something happened that you would find very interesting: The

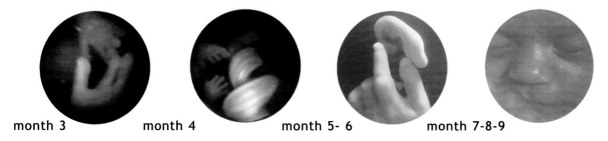

month 3 month 4 month 5- 6 month 7-8-9

information in the cell did not divide into two. That means the same information was duplicated in the two cells. After this, the cells continued to divide and the same information duplication happened in all of them, resulting in many cells with the same information. Then these were divided into others, and others divided into others. This event continued until millions of cells formed.

While all this was happening, something you would never guess took place!

These cells, although they contain the same information, started doing tasks that are different from each other. Some of them formed your brother's skin. Some others formed his muscles, yet others his skeleton, and others his brain neurons.

While the cells continued to multiply, the group of cells that was almost like a ball started to take shape. As you can see in the pictures at the top of the page, first your brother's head appeared, followed by his thin arms and then his legs. The cells continued to grow and divide and after nine months, they turned into a complete baby. You met him for the first time when he was "born".

All the things that we have said until now may surprise you. You probably have thought about why cells took on different tasks or how they were able to combine in such a neat shape. Allah is the One Who does all of this. Cells are tiny beings that are invisible to the

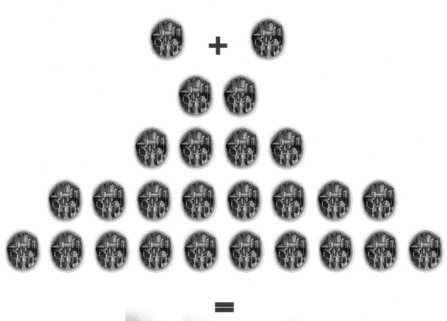

naked eye. Like atoms, it is impossible for cells all on their own to make decisions or to come together to form a human being. It is nonsense to even think that your brother or other human beings are made up of cells that came together by coincidence.

Allah, the Creator of all, has created all human beings perfectly and He has told the people to think about this in the Book that He has sent us:

Does not man recall that We created him before when he was not anything? (Surah Maryam: 67)

You, like your brother and all other human beings, started to grow from a single cell, continued to grow and turned into a full person. Right now, you are living a nice life in this world. You owe all of this to Allah. Allah shows great mercy to you and gives you many blessings. So, don't ever forget to thank your Creator, Allah.

HERE IS OUR BODY!

Our bodies are perfect organisms that allow us to live on earth in comfort, to run and play, to read and write and, in short, they let us perform each and every task. These organisms are so wonderful that one cannot make anything that resembles them even with the most advanced technology.

How much do you know about this body of yours, which works non-stop and repairs itself when it runs down?

WATER

PROTEIN

CARBOHYDRATES

MINERALS

SOLIDS AND LIQUID FATS

Did you know that your body is made up of fats, proteins, water, carbohydrates and minerals?

OUR WINDOWS ON THE WORLD: EYES

Each organ in our bodies is very important to us. Our lives would change if even only one of them were missing. For example, our eyes... Did you ever think what you would have done if you didn't have your eyes? You wouldn't be able to know what your parents, brothers or sisters, or friends look like. You wouldn't be able to see all the beautiful things. You wouldn't be able to play most of the games you now do. You wouldn't be able to read this book or see the colourful pictures in it. You wouldn't be able to imagine what a rabbit or a dog looks like, because you would never have seen one. You wouldn't be able to watch cartoons on TV. You wouldn't be able to perform your tasks with ease. You might not even be able to find your way around home. You wouldn't be able to see any colours or shapes, nor would you know what light is or be able to notice any of these things. The list is endless.

Allah created all humans with eyes with which they can see. Allah has given humans this very important asset.

Our eyes serve very important functions. They perform critical processes of which we are completely unaware, and only after which we can see around.

Let us briefly examine how we see:

Every object in the world reflects and emits light on to its surroundings. For instance, while you are looking at this book, the light reflected and emitted from this book is going to the back of your eye through your pupil.

This light, after going through a series of processes at the back of your eye, turns into an electrical signal. This electrical signal goes to your brain. At the back of your brain is the centre of vision that makes it possible for you

28

vision is a small area. This is the tiny area where the electrical signals form the image of the book and that is when you see this book.

Even trying to explain these processes as briefly as possible takes such a long time, whereas the process is instantaneous. These processes happen so fast that when you look at the book, at that instant you are able to see it.

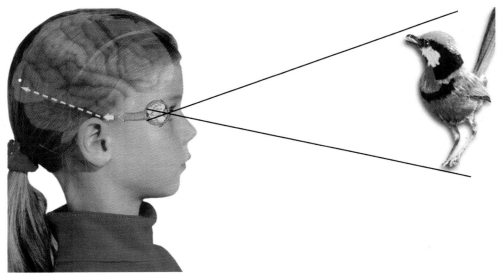

Isn't it such a perfect system? If you remember, we had mentioned evolutionists earlier in the book. We also mentioned that these people believe that earth, the universe, the stars and all living things are a result of chance. Those who say this say the same about our eyes. They say, "The eyes occurred by themselves and through coincidence." Can such a complex and wonderful system form by itself? Let us give an example to clarify how ridiculous this opinion is:

Engineers have manufactured the photographic and video cameras by copying the human eye. However, none of this equipment gives as clear a view as your eyes do. Now lift your head from the book and look around you. Isn't your vision clear? There is no blur, snowy dots or missing lines in your vision. Now look at your television set. Quite often, you see snowy dots or skipped lines in the image. Even when these don't happen and even with all the new technology, televisions still do not produce the perfect images that your eyes do.

Now, let's think for a moment. This means that our eyes are a lot more advanced and are of better quality than any video or photographic camera or television. What would you do if someone came up to you and said something like the following?

"There was a storm that caused some electrical cables, screws, hammers, screwdrivers to fly out the

door and windows, to fly out of the house, and then all of them got together in the backyard. Then there was some rain and thunder and these things were mixed with the soil. Some time passed and I saw a television set emerge. I picked it up and brought it home."

You would probably think that that person is either insane or lying, because as we all know, television sets are made in huge factories where there are hundreds of engineers, designers and specialised personnel. It is impossible for a television set to form on its own.

Could it be that our eyes, which are of much better quality than television, have occurred by themselves? Of course not! Just as a television doesn't come about on its own, but someone does manufacture it, our eyes are also not a result of coincidence. Allah is the One Who created our eyes in such a way that they see in three-dimensions and with coloured images so clearly. This is why we have to thank Allah for everything beautiful that we are able to see.

OUR EARS THAT HEAR WITHOUT ANY CRACKLE

Allah has created our ears perfectly just like our eyes. Imagine a stereo, for instance. Even if you turn on the best of stereos, you hear some crackling and hissing sounds. Radio channels often become mixed up. Right now, don't talk but just listen! Do you hear any hissing? Your ears never produce any. You hear the sounds marvellously clearly. Well don't you think that your ears could also have produced crackling just like stereos? Allah has created our ears perfectly and we are able to hear the sounds around us without experiencing any distortion.

Allah has created our ears in such a way that we are unable to hear certain sounds that would disturb us. The blood in our body, for instance, flows very fast and it makes a lot of noise during its circulation. However, our ears do not hear the noise that it makes. Our planet also produces

quite a strong noise while it spins. Nevertheless, Allah has created our ears so ideally that we don't hear this noise. Allah is very caring towards us. This is the reason why, throughout our lives, He doesn't let us hear noises that will disturb us.

This is why we have to thank Allah for His benevolence. Allah has stated the following in a verse in the Qur'an:

"Allah brought you out of your mothers' wombs knowing nothing at all, and gave you hearing, sight and hearts so that perhaps you would show thanks." (Surat an-Nahl, 78)

● ● ● ● ● ● ● ● ● ● ● ● ● ● ● ● ● ●

Here is a diagram that shows the inside of your ear. Your earflap collects the sounds, and the sound finally reaches the centre of hearing in your brain by moving inside your ear. And it is there that your hearing takes place.

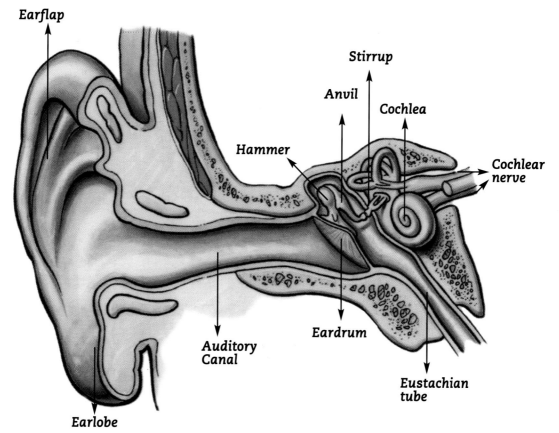

Earflap
Stirrup
Anvil
Cochlea
Hammer
Cochlear nerve
Auditory Canal
Eardrum
Eustachian tube
Earlobe

OUR HEART THAT NEVER TIRES

For us, our heart is an essential organ. It beats about seventy-two times per minute and about forty million times per year. To understand what a tiring activity this is, just make a fist with your hand and then relax it, and continue making a fist and relaxing it. How many minutes do you think you will be able to keep this up?

Your heart, which is about the size of your fist, continues this action throughout your life without becoming tired or even stopping once. Our hearts don't stop even while we are asleep. If we become excited, our heart beats faster, and it beats slower while we rest. Our heart makes all these adjustments automatically while we are totally unaware.

Every time our heart beats, it pumps blood around our bodies. What we need to survive is in this blood. Every one of our cells receives the necessary oxygen and food they need from the blood. Our heart pumps about 43,000 litres (approx. 11,000 gallons) of blood per day. Do you know just how much blood this means? This is about enough to fill 150 bathtubs. Wouldn't you become tired if you tried to empty a single bathtub full of water with just a cup? Now imagine having to empty 150 bathtubs of water with just a single cup. Probably you wouldn't have been able to accomplish such a difficult task. However, our heart does such a task

and has done so since the day we were born and will continue to do so until the day we die. Moreover, it never takes a break. You, for example, would take a break while doing a difficult chore. You would probably need to lie down, or take a rest, but our hearts don't become tired, because they are essential for our survival. It is small but its task is enormous. This is why Allah has created it in such a way that it never tires.

Blood cell

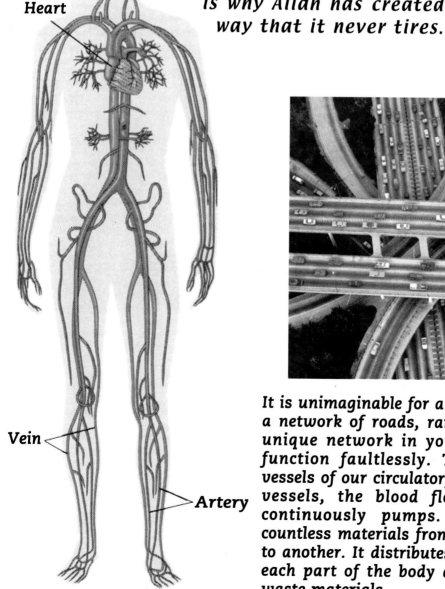

Heart

Vein

Artery

It is unimaginable for a country to be without a network of roads, railways or seaways. A unique network in your body allows it to function faultlessly. These are the blood vessels of our circulatory system. Inside these vessels, the blood flows that the heart continuously pumps. The blood carries countless materials from one part of the body to another. It distributes food continuously to each part of the body and collects waste materials.

35

DO YOU KNOW THAT THERE IS AN ARMY IN THE BODY THAT PROTECTS US AGAINST GERMS?

The places where we sit, the air we breathe, the things we hold are full of germs and viruses, but we are unable to see them. Germs and viruses are small organisms that cause diseases in human beings. We cannot see them with our eyes but they can cause us to become sick and to lose strength.

There are other organisms we are unable to see. These make up the army that lives inside us and protects us against our germ and virus enemies. This army is called the "Immune System".

Our immune system exists within our blood. The cells that make up our immune system are called the white blood cells.

When an enemy enters our body, our blood works just like a laboratory. It immediately produces very special substances to fight the enemy and reproduces more cells matching the enemy's strength. A ferocious battle begins. Sometimes the army in our body wins the battle without us feeling it and the germs and viruses die.

The importance and benefits of vaccination: Dangerous germs are given to the body after being made ineffective. In this way, the immune cells recognise them and take measures to protect you against them.

Enemy	Engulfer	Guard	Killer	Weapon Manufacturer	Weapon	Suppressor	Memory

The white blood cells, approximately more than a trillion, form a very advanced army. Each one of this army's personnel has its unique job. Some of them monitor whether there are any foreign bodies entering the blood stream, while others form the chemical substances that will destroy the enemies and others attack the enemy.

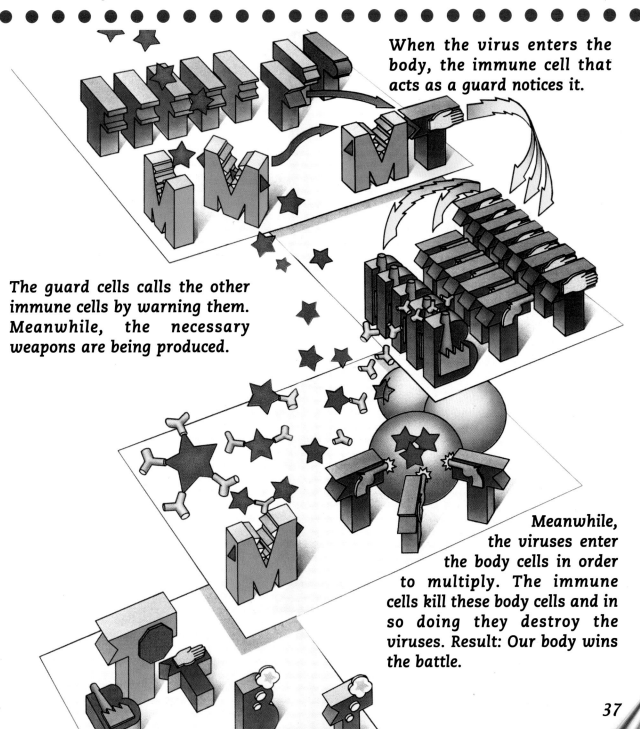

When the virus enters the body, the immune cell that acts as a guard notices it.

The guard cells calls the other immune cells by warning them. Meanwhile, the necessary weapons are being produced.

Meanwhile, the viruses enter the body cells in order to multiply. The immune cells kill these body cells and in so doing they destroy the viruses. Result: Our body wins the battle.

37

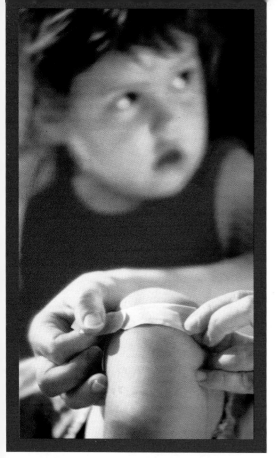

While you wear a bandage to protect yourself, the soldiers inside you fight for you.

Sometimes we do feel this battle. You say how? When we have a fever! Of course, you must have had a fever at least a couple of times by now. That was when your enemy was fighting the army inside your body. During the battle, your body uses up all its energy and needs some more. If you go out to run, while your body is engaged in a battle, you would be using up all the energy that your body needs to fight. In this case, your army would lose the battle and you would fall sick. However, when you get a fever, you naturally lie down to rest, and your army uses all your available energy. In doing so, the army could be victorious. When our temperature rises, our body gives us the message "rest!"

Do you know what would have happened, if we did not have an immune system? Shortly after we were born, the first germ that entered our body would have killed us. Because Allah is very merciful and caring towards all humans, He has created each human being with an immune system. As we have realised from the beginning of this book, we owe Allah each minute of our lives for our being able to see beautiful things and being able to eat delicious food. That is why we have to think about Allah in everything we see and say "O Allah, I am grateful to You for giving me all these blessings".

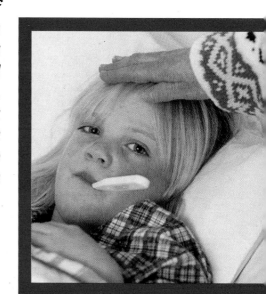

THE AMAZING FEATURES OF THE CREATURES AROUND US

Did you know that the living things that you see everyday have very interesting features?

After creating earth, Allah created many living things on it. One of these living things is the human being. We told you earlier how the human being was created. There are beings other than humans on this planet. These are the animals and plants.

In this section, we will explain the amazing features of some of these animals and plants. Some of these could be animals that you see everyday when you are out for a walk, playing in the backyard or sitting on the terrace. You probably haven't given a lot of thought to their unique features.

When Allah creates people, He gives them some features to constantly remind them of Him. For example, you can see the pictures of a human and a mosquito on this page. The mosquito is thousands of times smaller than the human. But, no matter what, the human is totally defenceless against the mosquito while sleeping in bed. Whatever she does, she will not be able to prevent the mosquito from biting. Allah has given the mosquito many special features, even though it is a lot smaller than the human being. As a result of this, He wants humans to ponder. He wants them to understand that humans can do nothing, even against a mosquito, without His wish. In this way, human beings should realise that they have absolutely no power in front of Allah.

Now, think about yourself. You go to bed and hear a continuous buzz. This is the buzz of a mosquito. As you can see in the picture the mosquito itself is tiny, but its noise is very strong. This is due to a unique talent that Allah gave it. However, do you know why the mosquito is trying continuously to bite you? Come on now; let's tell you about the interesting adventure of a mosquito.

A mosquito at work! In the bottom picture, can you see how the abdomen of the mosquito reddens as a result of the blood that it sucks?

THE AMAZING ADVENTURE OF THE MOSQUITO

Mosquitoes are creatures with which most humans are familiar because of their visits to our homes during the summer.

Did you ever get the chance to look at a mosquito closely? If not, look at the picture on the previous page and we can study it together. Do you know why the abdomen of this mosquito is red? His abdomen is red because it is filled with the blood of the person on whom the mosquito has landed. Why do mosquitoes suck blood? Many people believe that the mosquitoes feed on blood. In reality, mosquitoes feed on flower nectar.

The female mosquito is the only one that sucks blood, and that is for the sake of the eggs that she carries.

After learning this, you will probably view mosquitoes with different eyes. There are things about mosquitoes that will surprise you even more. As you know mosquitoes are creatures that live on land and that fly, but they grow in water and after they mature, they come out of the water without even getting wet. Did you ever hear of this incredible story? If you did not, then read on and you will be quite surprised.

The Adventure Begins...

The adventure of the small mosquito begins when the mother mosquito leaves her eggs on ponds or wet leaves. Yet, she doesn't leave her eggs at random. She aligns them neatly side-by-side. The eggs resemble a raft. Do you know why

The mother mosquito links her eggs in the shape of a raft to prevent them from sinking.

the mother mosquito arranges her eggs in this shape?

She gives her eggs this shape because, since they have been left on water, the eggs could easily sink. If they are linked in this way, the risk of sinking will no longer be there. The white eggs that the mother lines up with care immediately begin to darken. Insects and birds don't notice these eggs because their colour is dark. In this way, the eggs are safe from being attacked by insects and birds. So, from where does a tiny mosquito egg learn to change its colour?

Obviously, this tiny egg couldn't have this knowledge. The mosquito that is the mother of this egg also can't know how to change its colour. Allah is the One Who changes the colour of the eggs. Allah is very merciful and is the Protector of the living things He creates. He changes the colour of the mosquito eggs to protect them.

Wait! The mosquito's adventure has only just begun. The little ones inside the egg soon turn into wormlike creatures called larvae. These larvae, as you can see on the next page, stay in water with their heads upside down. How do you think these larvae breathe when their heads are in water? Allah has created them with an organ that allows them to breathe. Do you know what this organ looks like? It looks like the diver's snorkel the child in the next picture is using. This is a tube and the top of it stays out of water. The air that goes through this tube allows the tiny mosquito that is under water to breathe.

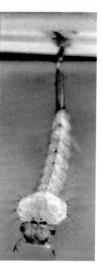

Mosquito larva

However, there is an important problem. This tube stays out of water but even the slightest wave could cause water to enter it and this would mean that the tiny mosquito would drown. This doesn't happen. A sticky substance at the end of this tube prevents water from entering it. Do you think that the larvae you see in the picture could have said, "Let's put a sticky substance at the end of our tube, so that water doesn't get inside"? Could little mosquitoes have such intelligence and talent? Obviously little mosquitoes cannot think of doing such things. Allah is the One Who creates the tube so that they can breathe and the sticky substance at the end of the tube so that water doesn't enter.

As you can see, Allah does not protect just you, He also protects all other living creatures.

Don't think that the adventure is over. It is still going on.

Meanwhile, the little mosquitoes change their skins a couple of times. Finally, they take the shape that you see on the left. It still doesn't look like a mosquito, does it? This phase of the mosquito is called the pupal stage. Inside the shell called the

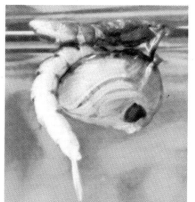

cocoon, the mosquito matures completely and takes the true shape of a mosquito. He becomes ready to fly with his antenna, mouth, feet, wings, and the eyes that make up a large portion of its head. But first, he must get out of the shell.

Mosquito cocoon

The mosquito that has come out of its cocoon is standing on water! Allah protects the mosquito from sinking with a sticky substance that He created for its feet.

The Mosquito is Out for the First Time!

The cocoon is first torn from the side of the head. However, the mosquito faces a very important danger before it is born. What if the cocoon fills with water? In that case, the mosquito would drown. However, the head portion of the cocoon is covered with a special sticky substance that prevents the head of the mosquito from coming into contact with water.

This is a very important moment, because the mosquito must stand on water on the tips of its feet, and it must not wet its wings. Even the slightest wind could cause the mosquito to tip over in the water and die. The mosquito manages this with great skill, because Allah created him with this talent.

How is the Mosquito Able to See You and Sting You at Night?

Did you ever wonder? It is dark at night and you are lying down on your bed. You are covered with your quilt. Only a little part of your arm is exposed. Yet the mosquito comes around in the darkness of night; it sees and stings that small part of you. So, while you are unable to see anything at night, how does the mosquito manage to see?

Mosquitoes are able to see the living things around them with the heat that they radiate, which is a kind of light invisible to us. Since this type of sight is not reliant on visible light, they can find our blood vessels even during the darkness of the night.

This is a unique talent. Due to this, scientists were able to invent a camera that captures images by means of heat. Even if it is dark, this camera images the surroundings as if it were daylight. Can you imagine? People copying a small mosquito! Could a mosquito possibly know more than a human, especially could it know more than a scientist? Of course not! Allah has given the mosquito extraordinary abilities. People are in awe of these extraordinary talents and try to copy them. They invented the aeroplane by copying birds. People have copied many other things after seeing them in nature. For now, let us continue the adventure of the mosquito.

The Mosquito at Work!

The technique that the mosquito uses to suck blood is so meticulous that it astonishes people.

First, the mosquito lands on a target. For

Mosquitoes see the living creatures around them according to their heat patterns. This is how a mosquito sees a group of people and then chooses its target.

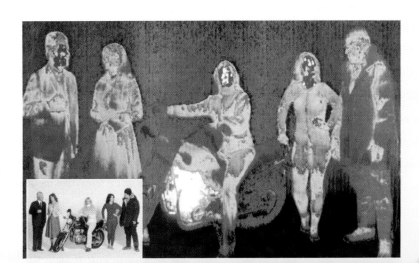

45

example, your arm... Then, with its needle-like tube, it chooses a suitable spot for itself. The needle of a mosquito resembles a syringe and it is protected with a special sheath. During blood suction, the needle is released from this sheath. Many people think that the mosquito pierces the skin by inserting its needle into it, whereas the mosquito uses a different method to do so. It moves its lower jaw back and forth, just like a saw and, with the help of its lower jaw, cuts the skin. It inserts its needle into this opening and when the needle reaches the blood vessel, it starts to suck blood.

Doctor Mosquitoes!

You could ask, "Can mosquitoes become doctors?" After reading this page you will say, "They really are doctors!"

When you get a cut, after a while, your blood stops dripping of its own accord. This is because blood can coagulate and stop flowing. Allah has created blood with this unique quality to protect human beings. If blood did not coagulate on its own, the tiniest cut on our finger or a wound from a fall while running could cause you to die since you wouldn't be able to stop the bleeding.

This is quite a vital benefit for us. However, mosquitoes might not be too happy about it. Why? Because, just when the mosquito starts to suck our blood, it would harden and not go up the mosquito's tube. If this were so, the mosquito would not have existed, because none of the mosquitoes would have been able to feed protein to their eggs. Again, Allah has created mosquitoes with a unique skill that is just right for this process. How? Before the mosquito begins to suck blood, it secretes a special liquid, given it by Allah, into the blood vessel of the person on whom it has landed. In this way, the blood in that area doesn't coagulate and so the mosquito is able to suck it.

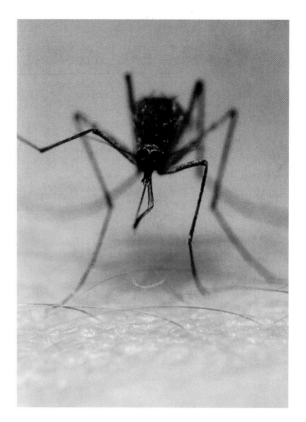

This liquid has another rare quality. While the mosquito does all these things, you won't feel a thing, because this substance numbs the area that the mosquito cuts. This liquid is just like a anaesthetic the dentist or surgeon uses. Doctors administer a certain drug so that you won't feel pain, and you don't. You see, the mosquito works just like a doctor. First, it anaesthetises and then it sucks.

After the mosquito bites you, you feel a little itching and swelling. The reason for this itching and swelling is this liquid.

You might think that all these things take a long time. The mosquito, however, manages most of these in a very short time. You feel the bite of the mosquito only after it has finished its job and packed away its equipment.

Now, let's think together. The mosquito is as large as the tip of a pencil, but the jobs it manages are very important and complex. Do you think that it is possible for a mosquito to think all of these things through? To prevent the flow of a human's blood, to anaesthetise the area that it cuts so that it doesn't cause pain, to make an eye *that can see easily even at night, to arrange its eggs in the shape of a raft so that they don't sink... It could not invent any of these, right?*

Allah has created every living being with the features most suitable for it so that they can feed themselves, protect themselves and survive. This shows just how caring, merciful and protective Allah is. If a mosquito is able to continue its life, for example, then this is because Allah is protecting it. Allah neither misses anything, nor does He forget. This is why everything that a mosquito needs is complete. Nothing is missing.

You can see in this picture, the course of action that a mosquito takes when it bites a human being. The mosquito does not suck blood to feed. It sucks blood only to feed its eggs. Furthermore, you won't feel a thing while the mosquito does these things, since the mosquito anaesthetises the area that it cuts.

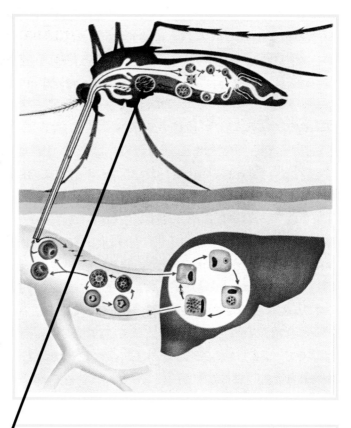

The mother mosquito feeds the eggs inside her with the blood that it sucks.

THE FLY IS ONE OF THE BEST FLYING CREATURES ON EARTH

We have so far mentioned the special features of the mosquito. In reality, all the insects that we see around us have interesting features. For example, flies are able to fly superbly from the moment that they are born. We can even say that, when it comes to flying, flies are the most talented creatures.

A fly can flap its wings about 500 to 1000 times per second. Stop here and think for a moment. The frame of time that we mention is not an hour and not a minute; it is just a second. That is, it is about the same time as the time in which you close and open your eyes. You see; the fly has flapped its wings at least 500 times while you closed and opened your eyes.

Now think about the following: What would you do if you were asked to open and close your arms only 10 times and not 500 times? Without a doubt it is impossible for you to manage this 500 times with the type of muscles your body has. The fly, with its extraordinary body muscles, manages this task that neither you nor mature adults can perform. Moreover, flies do not feel any difficulty while flapping their wings; their wing muscles do not wear out. This is because Allah has created them with such a magnificent system.

If you were to watch a fly closely, you would witness that it experiences no difficulty while taking off; this may not have seemed surprising to you and you may have taken this for granted. However, this is a very important and difficult move.

You know quite a lot about helicopters and aeroplanes. Well, do you know how long humans have been able to use them? The machines that are able to fly today were developed only during the last century. This means that a hundred years ago, there were no aeroplanes or helicopters like the ones that exist today. Engineers and technicians researched for a very long time; they worked for many years and developed this machinery only a short while ago. Look, this is very important: Today, none of the machines that fly have the complete ability to take off like flies do. This feature exists in some helicopters to some extent. However, even after all these lengthy efforts and the strong specially-developed engines, these helicopters still do not have the ability to fly as perfectly as flies.

Now, examine the first fly that you come upon. See what you notice: you will notice especially that the fly doesn't fly in a straight line. The fly can take off towards any destination it wants by making manoeuvres. It can, for example, zigzag in the air, and make abrupt turns. It can land on any surface, no matter how unsuitable. It can even land on ceilings or vertical walls with ease.

No flying machine can manage all these things. Try to imagine in your mind's eye the take-off of an aeroplane and a fly, and decide which one is more successful.

Now, this question may have occurred to you: Who teaches the fly all these moves? Again, what we see here is the presence of Allah the Most Powerful. Allah is the One Who has given the fly such immaculate flying ability.

When it comes to flying, even the helicopters that are manufactured by humans with the most advanced technologies are not as successful as flies.

THE TINY PRODIGIES THAT
PRODUCE HONEY

Do you know who makes the honey on your breakfast table?

You will probably reply, "yes!" We all know that bees make honey. However, do you know just how much these bees work to make the honey from the moment they are born until the moment they die, or just how giving and intelligent they are? Come on; let's study together how Allah has created the bees...

In a beehive, there is one queen, a few hundred male bees and a workforce of thousands of infertile female bees, the worker bees. (The total number of bees in the beehive can reach 80,000). The worker bees perform all the activities inside the hive. Some duties of the worker bees are as follows:

Building the honeycomb, cleaning and protecting the hive, feeding the queen bee and the male bees, caring for the bee larvae, and feeding them with the royal jelly, honey and pollen, building cells for the eggs to grow in, cleaning

these rooms, maintaining the heat and moisture inside the hive, collecting nectar, pollen, water and resin, etc.

We had mentioned earlier the life story of a mosquito. Now, let's take a look together at what type of life the worker bee leads.

A worker bee lives between 4 to 6 weeks. For 3 weeks after its birth it lives inside the hive. Its first job is to take care of the growing bees. It feeds the baby bees with the honey and pollen it takes from storage.

When the worker bee becomes 12 days old, suddenly, beeswax starts to be produced in its body. The beeswax is extremely important for bees, because the bees build their honeycombs with beeswax. You will see the picture of a honeycomb when you turn the page.

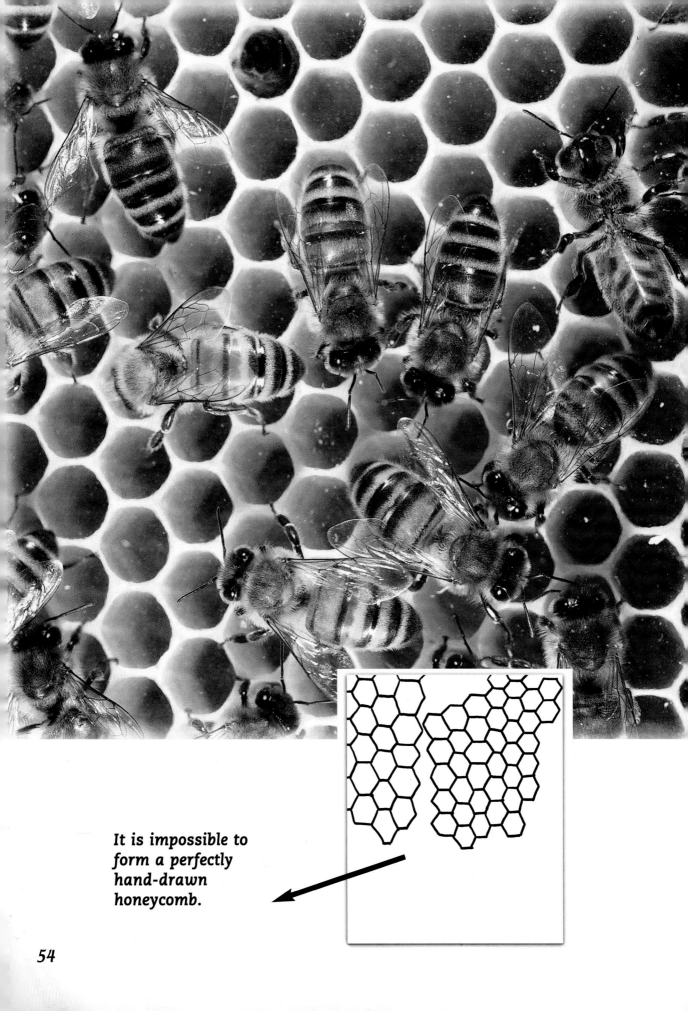

It is impossible to form a perfectly hand-drawn honeycomb.

Isn't it neat? Could you have made such neat hexagons side by side without a ruler? Furthermore, take a blank piece of paper and start to draw hexagons from one end of the paper while a friend starts to draw from the other. Were you able to come up with a neat honeycomb shape, right in the middle of the paper, without leaving any spaces? You weren't able to, right? This is something that even adults are unable to manage. Your teachers, parents, even your grandparents would not be able to achieve such a task. To be able to do this, you would need some instruments and you would have to do very complicated calculations. However, the tiny bee, even when it is just 12 days old, can make such a perfect honeycomb. What's more, it does this without using any instruments.

All the bees start making hexagonal honeycombs from the corners, and meet in the middle. You might have noticed that the honeycombs are the same height. How can a bee manage such tasks that even humans are not able to carry out and with such excellence? You see Allah is the One Who lets the bee do these things. Allah has created the bee with this talent.

The responsibilities of the worker bee are not just these. Among its duties, until it is 3 weeks old, are storing royal jelly and pollen in the honeycombs, keeping the beehive clean and throwing dead bees and garbage outside the beehive. During the last stage of its 3-week duty, it starts its last task of serving as a security guard and protecting the beehive from enemies. When the three weeks are over, the bee becomes skilled enough to collect royal jelly, pollen and water.

The worker bee becomes exhausted after working non-stop for another 2 to 3 weeks and dies.

During their brief lives, the bees work non-stop. In addition, no one teaches them the work that they are supposed to do. They start to work straight after birth. Just think, if a new-born baby were to get out of its bed, first make its bed, wash up, and then begin to take care of the other babies; wash them, feed them, dress them. Isn't this just impossible? Yet, bees manage such an impossible task, because Allah has created them with the capabilities to do so.

The Honey Bees that Dance

Did anyone ever tell you that bees have a dance? Some bees look for a food source outside the beehive. After flying about all day long, they find their own source and take with them as much royal jelly as they can, and then they return to their hive. There is still a lot more royal jelly left at the source but the bee cannot collect it all without the help of the other bees. The scout bee keeps the location of the food source in mind and quickly returns to the hive to gather its friends. It starts to make moves that

Bees dance by making movements resembling the figure "8". Their dance has a purpose: To show their co-workers the location of a food source.

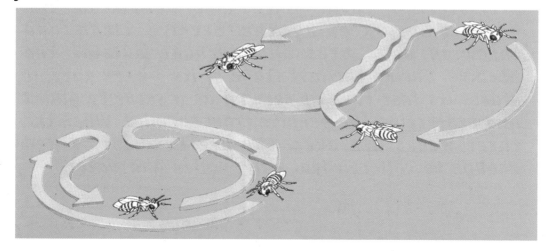

resemble the number 8 on the honeycomb. The numbers of times the bee turns or shakes its abdomen are signals that indicate the distance of the food source from the hive. By the end of the dance, the other bees have understood the location of the food source and they quickly leave for the flowers that are their new food source.

Where do you think tiny bees have learnt how to communicate by dancing? Of course, the One Who has given them this knowledge is their Creator and Protector, Allah.

Did You Know that Bees Make Honey for Us as Well?

Bees can produce much more honey than they need. As you know, bees make honey in their abdomens. Their tiny bodies make enough honey for themselves as well as for people.

But why are the bees so giving? Why don't they just make honey for themselves rather than thinking of our needs as well? Honey is very nutritious for people. This is the reason why Allah has created bees with the ability to make honey and has ordered them

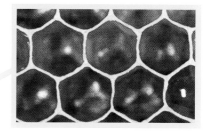

The bee stores honey in the cells it builds so perfectly. Here is the amazing honeycomb of the bee!

to make it in great quantities. Allah says in a verse in the Qur'an:

Your Lord revealed to the bees: "Build dwellings in the mountains and the trees, and also in the structures which men erect. Then eat from every kind of fruit and travel the paths of your Lord, which have been made easy for you to follow." From inside them comes a drink of varying colours, containing healing for mankind. There is certainly a Sign in that for people who reflect. (Surat an-Nahl: 68-69)

FASCINATING CREATURES

Until now, we only told you about the creatures that you are used to seeing around you. However, there are creatures that we don't usually see around us, but we come across in books or on television. These creatures also have very special features. We will now tell you about a few of these. Read all of them very carefully, because when you do, you will be very surprised, and at the same time you will say, "How wonderfully Allah has created them".

HOW DO PENGUINS LIVE ON SUCH A FREEZING CONTINENT AT THE SOUTH POLE?

Penguins live at the polar region of our planet. The unique feature of the pole is its amazing coldness and that it is always covered with snow and ice. The weather is so cold that it forms glaciers above the sea. Now, think about how cold you feel when you go out to play snowballs in the winter. You would feel cold even if you were wearing a sweater, a coat, a cap, a pair of gloves and a scarf. When you are playing snowballs, the temperature is probably only 10 degrees Celcius below zero (14 degrees Fahrenheit). The penguins live in a place where the temperature falls to 40° C below zero (-40° F).

Moreover, the penguins don't have any coats, sweaters or gloves, and they live in a place that is a lot colder than ours. They walk on ice without any shoes and they don't even become sick. They

South Pole

don't have homes. They sleep on ice. If you were to lie down on ice for even a few minutes, you would become seriously sick. Nothing happens to the penguins. Why?

It is because Allah has created them in such a way that they can live in such a freezing environment. Penguins' bodies and their features are very different from ours. Due to this, they can live in the coldest weather without any difficulties.

Allah has covered penguins' bodies with a very thick layer of fat, so that they won't feel the cold. The layer of fat prevents them from feeling the cold, and acts as a fur. Conversely, the layer of fat surrounding our bodies is quite thin and this is why we quickly become cold. This is why we have to wear thick clothes in cold weather.

The penguin displays great devotion towards its eggs and babies. Penguins incubate their eggs during the coldest weather. Unlike other creatures, it is not the female penguin that incubates the eggs but the male. The female penguin lays only one egg and then leaves it to the male. She leaves for distant places to find food for her husband and baby. Because of all the ice and snow that surrounds them, she has to travel far to be able to find food.

The male penguin incubates the egg for exactly four months. The penguin carries the egg in between his feet and during these four months, he never once leaves it on the ground. If he were to do so, the egg would freeze and die within a matter of minutes.

The male penguin is so patient that for four

months, he moves about with the egg between his feet. This is why he is unable to go hunting and remains hungry. The weather is very cold. When the weather becomes unbearably cold, all the male penguins get together even if they are carrying eggs between their feet. They come close to each other, forming a circle, and in this way, they warm each other up. They continuously switch positions so that the ones left outside the circle can also become warm. Just as the egg is about to hatch, the mother penguin returns from hunting. She feeds her baby with the food that she has stored in her throat. To prevent the baby from freezing, the mother and father penguins carry it in between their feet and keep it warm with the fur of their abdomen. As you can see, Allah has given these lovely creatures some exquisite features. Allah has created the penguin with a body that protects it from the cold, and has also made it very devoted. Because they are so dedicated, they take wonderful care of their offspring. This feature has been given to the penguins millions of years ago. The penguins that have lived before and the ones that are living now have not changed a bit when it comes to the devotion that they display.

When penguins go hunting, they leave their young in this position. The young penguins that keep close together don't become cold.

CAMELS CARRY WATER TANKS
ON THEIR BACKS

Just a while ago, we mentioned the penguins that live in the coldest part of earth, and how Allah has created them appropriately for that environment. On the other hand, camels are animals that were created to survive the hottest climates on earth. Camels are commonly used for transportation in the desert. Deserts are vast areas of sand and the temperatures in these areas can rise as high as 50⁰ C (122⁰ F).

You might have experienced temperatures around 30⁰ C (86⁰ F). Even at such a temperature, you immediately become tired and thirsty when you are out and playing.

Camels can still go for kilometres at temperatures of 50⁰ C (122⁰ F). They can stay without water for days. This is because Allah has also created their bodies very differently from ours. Camels store the water they drink inside them for long periods and they quench their thirst with the water they carry within them.

Feeding is also a problem in the

desert, since the desert is dry land and there is almost no vegetation. There are only cactuses and other thorny plants. The camel's mouth and lips are so tough that when it bites, it can even pierce a hole in the sole of a shoe. This is why it can easily feed on thorns and keep hunger away.

As well as that, the hair that covers the skin of the camel protects it from the intolerable heat. Allah has made the camel's feet wide because they always walk on desert sand. Due to their width, the camel's feet don't sink in the sand. In addition, Allah has made the skin under the camel's feet very thick. In this way, the soles of their feet never burn.

There are very frequent sandstorms in the desert. Did you ever witness a strong wind when you were at the beach? You would not have been able to open your eyes because you had to try to prevent all the sand from getting in them. If that wind were to become a bit stronger, you wouldn't have been able to see ahead. However, camels have two layers of eyelashes. These lashes weave into each other just like a trap and they protect the camel's eyes during sandstorms.

Allah has created every living thing with the features that are most suitable for their habitat. There are no penguins in the desert, for instance. Since the penguin's features are not suitable for desert conditions, the penguin would die quickly in the desert. Similarly, camels could not survive near the poles. Allah has created everything where they should be. Allah is the strongest and He has endless knowledge. Allah creates everything without any shortcomings. Allah informs us of the camel's creation in the Qur'an as:

"Have they not looked at the camel—how it was created?" (Surat al Gashiya: 17)

THE BEE HUMMINGBIRD

As you can see, this bird is small enough to stand on a pencil. Even with their small size, the bee hummingbirds travel very long distances and during this trip, they flap their wings around two and a half million times. Just how many times can you lift and put down your arms? If you try to lift them up and put them down only about 50 times, the next day your arms would ache. However, this tiny bird does this two and a half million times and nothing happens to it. Allah has created these birds with the ability to handle such an extremely difficult task.

THE DEFENSIVE CRAB: THE HERMIT

There are many interesting creatures living in the seas. These creatures mostly defend themselves by the most unusual methods. Hermit crabs, for instance, use live weapons to protect themselves from octopuses and other enemies. There is a type of vegetation that exists at the bottom of the ocean. The hermits collect these plants and put them on top of their shells. The reason for this is that these plants have thorns that are painful to the touch. In this way, the hermits protect themselves from their predators. Do not forget that hermit crabs could not have thought of such a brilliant plan all on their own. Allah has taught them how to protect themselves.

BOOBY, THE BIRD THAT SWIMS

Boobies are birds that dive into water from great heights, and they have webs between their toes. Allah has given them this flipper type of foot especially, so that they can swim on the surface and in the depths of the sea. Boobies dive as well. They dive into the sea to catch fish and they remain under the water to swim long distances.

DO FISH FLY?

Flying fish don't fly with wings like birds, but they slide on fins that resemble a bird's wings. They travel about 56 kilometres (35 miles) in an hour. These small fish can move faster in water by spreading their fins and lifting their tails out of the water. In this way, they slide swiftly in water.

Flying fish gain speed by spreading out their wing-like fins.

THE HERON

The heron displays great skill in catching fish. It stands up spreading its wings in an umbrella shape above its head. This produces a shadow and prevents reflections from the surface of the water. Now, the heron can clearly see its prey under the surface of the water. The wings of the bird form a circular shadow on the water's surface, and it always fishes inside this circle.

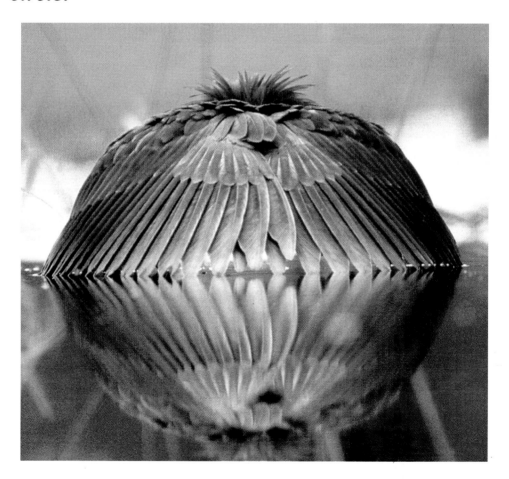

THE OSTRICH

The ostrich is a bird that runs extremely fast. It can run at speeds of up to 70 kilometres (45 miles) per hour. The ostrich has only two toes on each of its feet, and one of these toes is much larger than the other one. The uniqueness of the ostrich is its ability to run only on its big toe.

THE POLAR BEAR

The polar bear can run very fast on ice with his levelled, hairy claws and non-slippery soles. Polar bears, with their thick furs, have a very important protector in such cold polar weather. A 10 cm (4 inch) thick layer of fat prevents the cold from affecting them. This is why they can swim in icy cold waters with speeds of 10-11 km/hour (7 miles/hour), for distances of about 2000 km. (1250 miles). Allah has created polar bears, like penguins, so that they can survive in such cold habitats, and He has positioned them in the coldest parts of earth, at the poles, the polar bear at the North Pole and the penguin at the South Pole.

Allah has also given polar bears a very strong sense of smell. Their sense of smell is so acute that they can easily pick up the smell of a seal hiding beneath 1,5 metres (1,6 yards) of snow.

In addition, it has an extra eyelid that is like a membrane. This membrane acts as "a pair of sunglasses" and protects them against snow-blindness.

CHEETAH: THE FAST RUNNER

Cheetahs are known as the fastest running animals on land. They can go over short distances with great speeds. They can accelerate up to 75 km. (45 miles) per hour within a few seconds. Some cheetahs can run more than 600 metres (650 yards) at the unbelievable speed of 113 km/hour (70 miles/hour).

THE INTERESTING METHOD OF GAZELLES

Some creatures use the method of leaving scents to border their territories. For example, the gazelle uses long thin twigs and plants, as well as a substance, which smells like tar, secreted by glands directly under its eyes to mark its territory. This scent lets other gazelles know that this territory already has an owner. Reindeer, on the other hand, have scent glands on the tips of their rear feet. The substance secreted by these glands makes it possible for them to mark their territories. Rabbits mark their territory with a substance secreted by glands on their chins.

THE GECKO'S FEET SUCTION CUPS

The gecko is a type of lizard that lives in hot climates. Its most amazing feature is its ability to walk on vertical flat surfaces with ease. The geckos can easily climb even on glass with the help of the suction cups on the tips of their toes. In addition, they have hidden claws in their toes. When they reach uneven surfaces, they let out these claws just like a cat and continue their walk.

THE BASILISK THAT RUNS ON WATER

What would you think if you saw a lizard running on water? You could say, "I'm probably dreaming". This is not a dream; it is reality! The lizard, named the basilisk, can run on water and it can do this extremely fast. Flaps at the back of its feet allow it to splash the water. These flaps curl up when it walks on land. If it comes across any

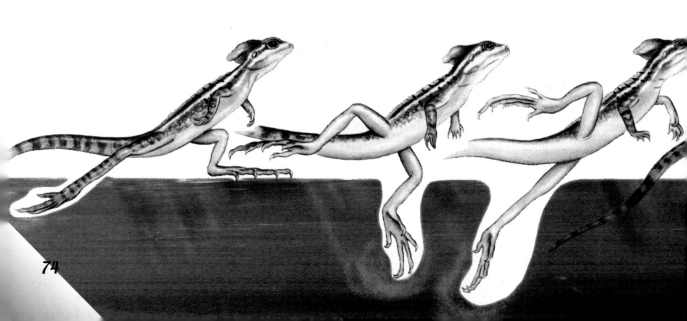

danger, it quickly gets into water and starts to run fast. Meanwhile, the flaps on the back of its feet open and provide it the width that will allow it to run on water.

DUCKS

Ducks can fly with speeds of up to 50 km. (30 miles) per hour. In addition, they keep on changing direction to protect themselves from predators. When they need to dive into water, they do it so fast that it becomes extremely difficult for hunters to hunt them down.

ELEPHANT'S LONG TRUNKS

The trunks of elephants contain 50,000 muscles. When needed, these muscles contract, making it possible for the elephant to push even the heaviest of loads. The trunk, at the same time, can perform such delicate tasks as collecting pea seeds and cracking them open in the elephant's mouth. The trunk, which is practical in so many ways, can also be used as a long finger, a trumpet or a loudspeaker. The trunk can hold about 4 litres (7 pints) of water for drinking or showering the body.

You may have heard these special features of the creatures we have mentioned for the first time. They all have very awesome features, don't they? These are only a few of the awesome creatures on earth. There are thousands of animals on earth like these that you might not have seen or heard of yet. Well, could all these animals have achieved such interesting features by chance? Of course not! Allah is the One Who has created them with all these features and unique qualities.

HOW DO COLOURFUL PLANTS EMERGE FROM SOIL?

Your parent prepares your meal everyday and brings it to the table. There are different types of vegetables and fruit on the table. Well, did you ever wonder where they all come from?

All plants, flowers, fruit and vegetables grow in dark soil. So, how do beautifully

scented red roses or strawberries, or wonderfully scented, water-filled yellow lemons emerge from the dark soil, which does not smell so good?

Each plant, vegetable, flower and fruit has different smells, colours and tastes. Apricots, peaches, watermelons, oranges, cherries, strawberries, bananas, grapes, and figs have each different taste, smell and shape. Allah has created them all for us. All of them are delicious, and at the same time, have the vitamins and the minerals that are essential for us. There are different fruits for winter and summer, each one meeting our needs. The oranges, tangerines and grapefruits, for instance, that come out in winter have an abundance of vitamin C. Vitamin C increases the strength of our body against the winter's cold. During the summer, juicy fruits such as watermelons, cherries, cantaloupe and peaches come out. In the summer, the weather becomes hot, causing our bodies to lose water, and we are able to replace this water with the help of these fruits.

None of these have happened by accident. The watermelon hasn't decided by itself, all of a sudden, to emerge during the summer. Neither did the tastes and smells of all of these fruits just happen. No fruit could decide its scent. Could an orange, for instance, decide, "let my scent be this", "let my colour be orange", "let me be sweet", "let me shield my pieces with a cover" and "let me divide into slices, so that people can eat me with ease"?

Of course not!

Allah creates fruit for people with such features that are more beneficial for them, so that they will continue to be strong and healthy, and enjoy the fruit they eat. For this reason, when we eat something we like, we must never forget that Allah created it and gave it to us. We must thank Allah for the beautiful things that He has given us and shown us.

LET'S THINK AGAIN!

So far, we have mentioned our planet, our bodies and the living creatures on earth. We asked, "How could all of these have occurred?" Just think, earth was created and there was nothing on it, and then all of a sudden living things appeared on it. In the seas, there were the fish and the seaweed, and on land humans, lions, cats and ants started to appear. A bird started to fly in the sky from nowhere. How could all of these creatures have suddenly appeared?

Obviously, Allah has created all of them.

Allah is the Creator of everything that we see around us.

Allah first created the universe and then our planet. After that, He created the animals, plants and human beings. It is very easy for Allah to create all of these, because He is very Powerful. Allah can do what He wants in an instant.

As we told you before, some people do not want to accept a truth that is so clear. These people called "evolutionists", say that, "everything happened on its own".

This is nonsense. What do you think when you come home and see a freshly baked cake? Do you not say, "Hmm, my mother has baked a cake"? This means that if there is something concrete we can see, then there must have been someone who made it.

Do you know what the lie that these evolutionists tell is like? It is just like saying, "No one baked that cake in the kitchen; it baked itself by accident". What would you answer if you heard this? You would probably say, "What nonsense, could a cake bake itself? Someone must have baked it." What if the person next to you still insists and says: "The screws of the kitchen cupboards became loose and the cupboards started to rock. During this rocking, the flour, butter, sugar and cocoa fell from them and mixed. They mixed in just the right proportions. That is to say that everything was just the right amount, the sugar, the cocoa... While the mix was falling off the cupboard, it just happened to directly fall into a baking dish that was standing exactly at the point of their fall. Just at that moment, an earthquake took place, and I don't know how the dish got into the oven, but it just did. Even all these coincidences are still not enough to bake the cake. There had to be another coincidence and that is that the oven had to be at the correct temperature setting. Right then, another thing happened by chance: the oven's dial turned on and then later it turned off by itself at the precise moment the cake was done, and so the oven turned itself off before the cake was burned."

Do you think that anyone would believe such a story? Of course, nobody would!

Then think for a moment: to form the sun, stars, seas, lakes, mountains, fish, cats, rabbits and human beings is a lot harder and more complex than producing a cake, but even a cake could not occur by itself through chance. Then to say that the sun or humans have come about on their own is very foolish. If there is someone baking the cake, then there is a very Intelligent Being Who has created the sun and humans. This Being is Allah, our Lord.

Throughout the second part of our book, we will talk about the evolutionists who don't believe in the presence of Allah and who say, "everything happened on its own". These people try to confuse others by saying things that are not true.

However, when a person says things that are not true, the falsehood that he tells becomes apparent. If the person across from him were smart, he would immediately understand that the other one is not telling the truth. These evolutionists have many loopholes in their tall tales. Let us see for ourselves how unbelievably nonsensical are the things they tell us and how apparent their falsehoods are...

WHAT IS THE THEORY OF EVOLUTION?

CHARLES DARWIN

People who do not believe in Allah have an idea. This idea is called the "theory of evolution". The people who believe in the theory of evolution are called "evolutionists".

The person who has proposed the theory of evolution was called Charles Darwin and he lived about 150 years ago. Darwin did not believe that Allah created all living things. According to him, everything happened on its own and purely by accident. He thought that creatures changed shape into other creatures and this is how all the creatures came about. This means, according to Darwin, that one day, fish turned into reptiles by chance. Another day by more luck, reptiles started to fly thus becoming birds. According to the story that Darwin proposed, humans were formed from apes. This means that, to Darwin, your ancestor was an ape! Now, to understand Darwin's tall tale better, go and view the pictures on the next page.

The evolutionists' claim is so ridiculous that it often becomes material for comic strips.

As we explained to you before, the tiniest part that makes up animate and inanimate things is the atom. This means that in reality, you are made up of billions of atoms that have come together.

When earth appeared for the first time, there were no creatures on it. There were only some inanimate things. Evolutionists—believers in Darwin—say that one day some of these atoms came together by chance. This means that there was a strong wind or maybe a cyclone one day

after earth was formed, and it helped these atoms come together. What happened to these atoms after that, you ask?

According to Darwin's story, these atoms joined to make cells. As you know, every living thing is made up of cells. The cells unite to make our eyes, ears, blood, heart, and in short, all of our body and the cells are very complex. It is impossible for something so complex to be made of atoms that have come together by chance.

In a cell, there are hundreds of different tiny organs. We could relate the cell to an enormous factory except that we have to remember that it is organic and not mechanical; it is just a way of speaking. If you pay attention to the picture on the next page, you will notice that it resembles a factory.

The cell looks like a very advanced factory with its production centres, transportation devices, storage department, and many other departments. There are many activities taking place in this factory. Some of the personnel inside the cell work as engineers and others as chemists or foremen. Don't ever forget: the cell is a structure that is so small, that it cannot be seen with the naked eye.

In a cell, there are manufacturers, transporters for the materials, entrance and exit gates, production centres, message carriers, energy control centres, etc. Well, do you think that it is possible for a factory to form all by itself, with stones, soil, and water coming together after a possible storm and all of it by chance? Of course not! Everyone would laugh at such a ridiculous claim. Nevertheless, evolutionists do make a claim that is just as ridiculous by saying, "the cell was formed by chance".

As stated in the evolutionists' allegation, these cells formed living things when they came together by some kind of luck.

THEN LET THE EVOLUTIONISTS CARRY OUT A DARWINIAN EXPERIMENT!

Let them get a huge barrel. Allow them to put inside this barrel all the atoms that they wish. Permit them to put inside the barrel whatever else their hearts desire. Let them put inside the barrel all the things necessary to make a living being. Then they can either warm up or electrify this barrel. Allow them to carry out whatever they want freely. They can keep watch over the barrel for millions of years. (They can pass the task to younger evolutionists, as their lifetimes would not be enough.)

What would happen as a result of all this?

Do you think that lambs, violets, cherries, bunnies, bees, melons, cats, dogs, squirrels, roses, plums, strawberries, fish, elephants, giraffes, and lions could come out of this barrel? Could a person who thinks, becomes joyful, becomes excited, enjoys listening to music and reading books come out of this barrel?

Of course not!

Neither could anyone like the professors keeping watch over the barrel emerge. Not only could a professor not emerge, not even one of the professor's trillions of cells could emerge.

Atoms are lifeless. Can lifeless matter link together to produce a living, laughing, thinking being?

Could an intelligent person believe such a thing? Of course, no living thing could come out of that barrel. That is impossible, because living things aren't made up of lifeless matter coming together by coincidence. Allah created all living things. Allah decided to create humans, mountains, lakes, lambs, lions, and flowers when there was nothing around, and He has created everything from nothingness just by giving the order "Be!"

calcium
fluorine
iron
manganese

phosphorus
copper
zinc

sodium
magnesium
chromium
selenium

potassium

iodine
molybdenum

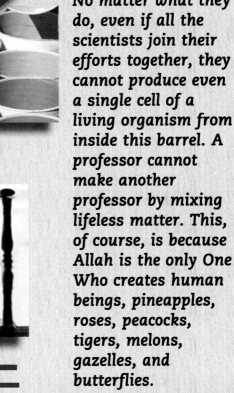

Only these materials are needed for the Darwinian experiment, because evolutionists claim that the substances such as iodine and zinc that you see above came together by chance to make living things. So, let them come and mix all of these substances together inside a huge barrel. Allow them to do to it whatever they want. After that, let them wait for as long as they want.

No matter what they do, even if all the scientists join their efforts together, they cannot produce even a single cell of a living organism from inside this barrel. A professor cannot make another professor by mixing lifeless matter. This, of course, is because Allah is the only One Who creates human beings, pineapples, roses, peacocks, tigers, melons, gazelles, and butterflies.

HOW, ACCORDING TO EVOLUTIONISTS, DO LIVING THINGS EVOLVE?

As stated by the theory of evolution, a living thing evolves with time, that is to say, it develops other features, and then turns into another living being. For instance, according to evolutionists' belief, a reptile, as a result of some events, evolves into a bird. So, what are these events that they claim cause the reptile to change into another creature?

Evolutionists believe that evolution takes place as a result of two separate events that occur simultaneously, called "mutation" and "natural selection". This, actually, is an illogical belief and it does not have any scientific basis. "Why?" you say. Let us see why, together.

WHAT IS NATURAL SELECTION?

The simplest explanation for natural selection is that the strongest creatures survive, whereas the weak disappear.

Let's explain this with the following example:

We will say, for instance, that there is a herd of deer and that predators are constantly attacking this pack. In this case, the deer will start to run fast and only the fastest running and most agile deer will survive. In time, weak and slow deer will completely disappear, as the predators hunt them down. There would only be healthy and strong deer in existence. Therefore, after some time, the deer pack would only consist of strong deer.

ANTELOPES RUNNING AWAY FROM CHEETAHS...

WOULD NOT CHANGE INTO A TIGER WHILE RUNNING...

AND TIGERS WOULD NOT CHANGE INTO ELEPHANTS!!!

The events we have mentioned until this moment are correct, but they have nothing to do with evolution. Evolutionists say that a deer, after continuously evolving, would turn into another living thing, a giraffe, for example. This is wrong, because no matter how fast a deer runs, or how long it extends its neck upward, it cannot turn into another creature, a lion or a giraffe, for example. This can only happen in fairy tales. You probably all know the story about the frog that turns into a prince. A frog can turn into a prince only in a fairy tale. However, it is impossible for a deer to change into a lion or another living thing in real life. However, evolutionists—although most of them are adults and possibly even scholars and professors—believe in such a story! Do you know what this is like? It is as if a child, who has just listened to the fairy tale of the frog that turns into a prince, picks up a frog, kisses it and waits for it to become a prince.

We can conclude that: Natural selection can never change a species of animals into another species, for example a deer into a lion or a giraffe. It can only cause the members of that animal species, a herd of deer for instance, to become stronger.

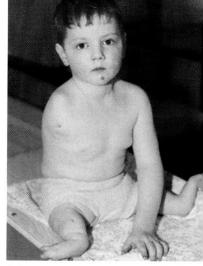

WHAT DOES MUTATION MEAN?

Mutations are the adverse changes that take place in a living organism's body. Radiation or chemical substances cause mutations. The effects of radiation and chemical substances on living things are always harmful. About 55 years ago, during the Second World War, an atom bomb was dropped on the Japanese city of Hiroshima. The atom bomb spread radiation around the area and this caused a lot of harm to people. The radiation caused most of the people either to become seriously ill or die. Moreover, it destroyed some bodily systems of the exposed people, and this in turn caused their children to be born either sick or crippled.

Mutations are harmful events that have made a child like this.

Another such event took place in the Russian city Chernobyl in 1986. There was an explosion at the Chernobyl nuclear plant, and this caused radiation to spread over the whole city, surrounding areas and even as far as Western Europe. Just as in Japan, the people who were living there at the time and their children who were born subsequently either became crippled or died of radiation.

A lamb that ended up with five legs due to a mutation.

The pictures that you

People whose feet have been damaged as a result of mutations.

have seen all show how people and other living things have been crippled after mutating as a result of radiation.

You could ask what does this have to do with our topic? We mentioned earlier that evolutionists claim that living things turned into other species and this is how they evolved. They, for instance, say that fish turned into reptiles.

If you were to ask, how can a fish turn into a reptile, they would reply: One day a fish mutates, that means that it goes through an event just like the children in Japan who were exposed to radiation. Because of this mutation, the body of the fish goes through some changes and one day, millions of years later, you would come across a crocodile that used to be a fish!

This claim is nonsense. Furthermore, as we mentioned above, mutations are always harmful to living creatures. They either cripple them or make them very sick. Nonetheless, the theory of evolution still maintains that mutations have caused the fish to evolve and changed them into reptiles. This is just too fantastically unbelievable for anyone to believe.

If mutations were beneficial, when the radiation leak occurred, everyone would have gone to Chernobyl to evolve into more advanced beings. In fact, everyone has fled from Chernobyl, and the adverse affects of Chernobyl incident are still evident.

We can compare evolutionists' claims with the following example: If you took hold of an axe and hit a black and white television with it, could you change this television into a coloured one? Of course not! If you randomly hit a television with an axe, you would end up with a smashed set. Just as hitting

IF YOU HIT A BLACK AND WHITE TELEVISION WITH AN AXE...

YOU COULD END UP WITH A COLOURED TELEVISION !!?

WRONG! MY TELEVISION SET IS SMASHED...

something haphazardly with an axe produces damage, mutations harm living beings.

That is to say, mutations don't turn a living creature into something better, as evolutionists argue.

Then, let us summarise what we have mentioned until now: Evolutionists claim that a creature evolves into another creature or a species into another species. They say that these changes occur as a result of two things, mutations and natural selection, but we have already seen that neither natural selection nor mutation can change the features of a living being. Furthermore, mutations cause damage to living beings, as we have seen in the pictures.

A 100 million-year-old fossil of an ant. As you can see, ants a hundred million years ago were just like the ants of today. That is to say, they have not evolved!

FOSSILS THAT EVOLUTIONISTS JUST CAN'T SEEM TO FIND

What is a Fossil?

A fossil is a part of an animal or a plant that has been dead a long time—usually thousands of years. It is preserved in rock formations in the earth's crust. In order for a plant or an animal to become a fossil, it must be buried almost immediately after it dies. For example, if there was a bird on the ground and a heap of sand suddenly fell on it causing it to die, the remains of this bird could have survived to the present day. Similarly, there is a resin of some trees that becomes fossilised by geological processes and is then called "amber". Sometimes this resin flowed over bugs, and the bugs died inside the resin. In this way, it solidified, and amber and bugs have been preserved without damage for millions of years until our time. Thus, we can learn about creatures that lived long ago. These remains of the creatures are called fossils. You can see some of these fossils in the following pages.

What Does "A Transitional Form" Fossil Mean?

The most important falsehood that evolutionists invent is the "transitional forms". In some evolutionist books, these are sometimes called "intermediate transitional forms".

As you know, evolutionists claim that creatures evolve from each other. They state that the first creature came about by chance. In time, that creature changed into another, and that other creature turned into another creature and so on. Let us illustrate this with an example: Evolutionists say that fish, for example, have come from a creature that resembles a starfish. This means that one day, due to mutation, a starfish lost one of its arms, and during the next millions of years it lost all of its arms except for some that started by themselves to develop into fins. Meanwhile and simultaneously, all the other changes that are necessary for a starfish to change into a fish took place. (It is impossible for something like this to happen but we are just putting together a scenario!). According to the tale of evolutionists, a starfish has to go through many phases to turn into a fish. If you look at the drawing below you will understand better just how absurd this claim is.

Imaginary transitional forms

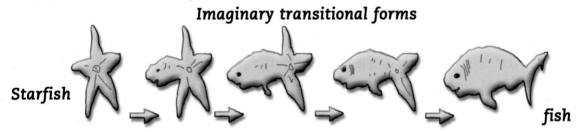

Starfish

fish

Creatures that were passing phases between definite species are called transitional forms. Moreover, according to the theory of evolution, these creatures all ought to have had half-complete organs. Furthermore, there ought to have been many later transitional forms such as fish that turned into reptiles, as they suggest. These in-between species would have to have had half feet, half fins, half lungs and half gills. If these creatures had really existed then we should be able to find their remains, namely their

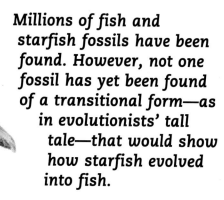

Millions of fish and starfish fossils have been found. However, not one fossil has yet been found of a transitional form—as in evolutionists' tall tale—that would show how starfish evolved into fish.

A 50 million-year-old-fish fossil

A 100-150 million-year-old starfish fossil

In the above pictures, you can see fish and starfish fossils along with pictures of how they look today. As you can see, neither of them has changed one bit. They are just as they were millions of years ago.

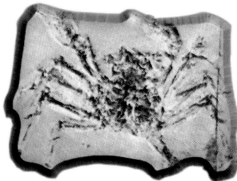

A 150 million-year-old crab fossil

Can you see any difference between the two crabs?!

fossils, but it is extremely interesting that so far we have been unable to find fossils of any of the transitional forms that evolutionists claim existed.

Fossils are scientific proof. This means that by looking at fossils, we can learn how creatures lived long ago. Fossils show us that: Creatures have not evolved from each other, but that they have all been formed at some instant without any feature missing and without defect, and they are no different from their like that are alive today. Allah created them all.

A MODERN SEA URCHIN AND A 125 MILLION-YEAR-OLD SEA URCHIN FOSSIL

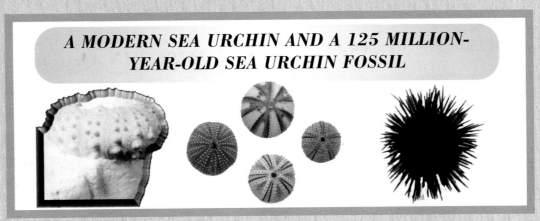

A MODERN CROCODILE AND A 190 MILLION-YEAR-OLD CROCODILE FOSSIL

A MODERN RAY FISH AND A 75 MILLION-YEAR-OLD RAY FISH FOSSIL

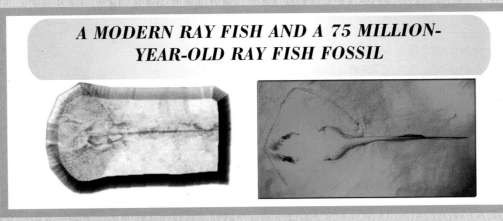

A MODERN SHARK AND A 400 MILLION-YEAR-OLD SHARK FOSSIL

MODERN GRASSHOPPERS AND A 40 MILLION-YEAR-OLD GRASSHOPPER FOSSILISED IN AMBER

A MODERN GECKO AND A 90-94 MILLION-YEAR-OLD GECKO FOSSILISED IN AMBER

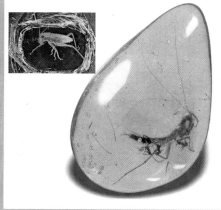

A MODERN FROG AND A 90-94 MILLION-YEAR-OLD FROG FOSSILISED IN AMBER

You see fossils of some creatures on these pages. Next to them are pictures of the same creatures as they are today. As you can see, no changes have occurred in these creatures for millions of years. Today, they are still as on the first day Allah created them. None of them have evolved into other species.

A MODERN NAUTILUS AND A 450 MILLION-YEAR-OLD FOSSILISED NAUTILUS

Evolutionists cannot explain how these creatures remained exactly the same for millions of years.

A MODERN TORTOISE AND A 50 MILLION-YEAR-OLD TORTOISE FOSSIL

A MODERN SHRIMP AND A 195 MILLION-YEAR-OLD SHRIMP FOSSIL.

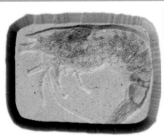

A MODERN DRAGONFLY AND A 150 MILLION-YEAR-OLD DRAGONFLY FOSSIL

WHAT HAPPENED DURING THE CAMBRIAN PERIOD?

We had mentioned earlier that it is now thought that Allah created the universe in the big bang. The whole universe, planets, stars and our own earth were formed after this enormous explosion.

To begin with, there were no livings beings on our planet, but then Allah created all living things on earth; birds, insects, trees, flowers, fish, tigers, butterflies, elephants and giraffes etc.

Well, do you know when the first living creatures appeared? This happened during the period called the Cambrian about 500 million years ago. The first creatures that lived during this period were ones like snails, worms and starfish. The creatures that lived during the Cambrian period also prove that the theory of evolution is completely wrong. How come?

These creatures appeared all of a sudden during the Cambrian period. Before them, no other living beings existed on the planet. The fact that these creatures appeared out of nowhere and all of a sudden is proof that Allah created them in an instant. If the theory proposed by evolutionists were right, then these creatures must have evolved gradually from simpler ancestors. However, these creatures have neither ancestors nor any transitional forms that lived before them. No fossil hunter (palaeontologist) has ever come across such a transitional form. Fossils show us that these creatures—just like all other living beings— suddenly appeared during the Cambrian period, without any features missing, and with no ancestors from whom they evolved. That is, Allah created them. Furthermore, these creatures that lived during the Cambrian period

had very special features. For example, there used to be a creature called the trilobite that lived during the Cambrian period, but we do not see them now because they are extinct. The Trilobite had very complex but perfect eyes. Its eyes, as you can see on the right, were made of hundreds of honeycomb-shaped cells and these cells allowed it to see very clearly.

Do you think that a creature like this could just appear out of nowhere? If your little brother came to you and said, "I was sitting at the table last night and out of nowhere a fly appeared in front of me. I don't know where it came from but all of a sudden, it was produced there by chance. It had very interesting honeycomb-shaped eyes. But these were probably made by chance too."

What would you think at such a moment? Probably you would think that your brother is too small to realise the complicated nature of life. However, what is so strange is that evolutionists say that these creatures suddenly appeared in the seas. The eyes of flies today are very similar to the eyes that these creatures had. In that case,

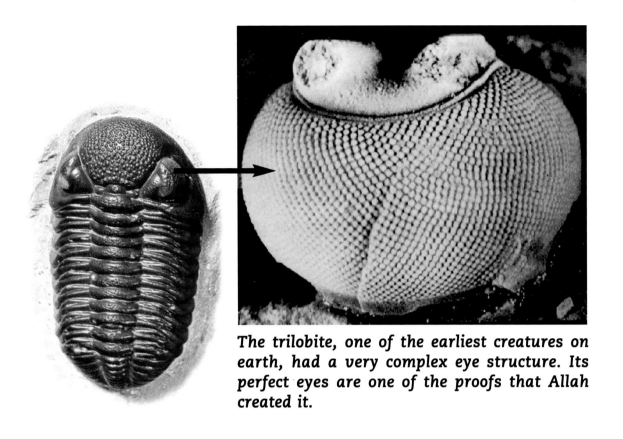

The trilobite, one of the earliest creatures on earth, had a very complex eye structure. Its perfect eyes are one of the proofs that Allah created it.

evolutionists are clearly wrong. Because they are so proud and arrogant, they do not want to admit that Allah has created all living things. They constantly fabricate stories, imaginary scenarios, and what are fairy tales to cover up the truth so that people move away from Allah.

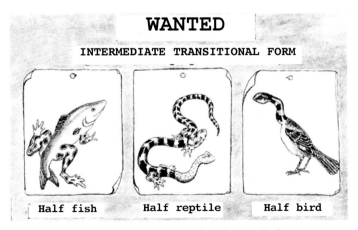

WANTED

INTERMEDIATE TRANSITIONAL FORM

Half fish   Half reptile   Half bird

The strange creatures that evolutionists claim once existed. In reality, such creatures have never lived.

THE FALSEHOOD THAT FISH CHANGED INTO REPTILES

Evolutionists say that reptiles evolved from fish. According to them, one day, when food in the sea was scarce, fish decided to look for some on land, and when they were there, they changed into reptiles to be able to survive on land. As you can see, this is an absurd idea, because everybody knows what would happen to fish if they went on land: They would die!

Did you ever go fishing? Just think! What would happen if a fish took the bait and was hooked on your line and you saved its life and brought it home to rest in your backyard? As we have just said, it would die. If you were to fish again, and this time caught many fish and brought them all to lie in your backyard, what would happen? Again, they would all die!

You see, evolutionists do not accept these things. They say that one of the fish in your backyard, while waiting for its death, started to change suddenly, and turned into a reptile and continued to live! Something like this is impossible!

Evolutionists claim that, fish decided to go ashore and changed into land creatures. In reality, fish that go ashore die!

104

It can never be possible because there are a lot of differences between fish and land creatures and all of these changes cannot just happen suddenly by coincidence. Let us list just a few of the things that fish would need to survive on land:

1. Fish use gills to breathe in water. However, on land they cannot breathe with their gills and so they would die. They would need to have lungs. Let us just suppose that a fish made up its mind to go on land, where would it get a lung from?

2. Fish do not have a kidney system like ours, but they need one to live on land. Probably they found kidneys lying somewhere when they decided to go on land!

3. Fish do not have feet. This is why they cannot walk when they reach shore. Just how did the first fish that decided to go on land find feet? As this is impossible, it is obvious that evolutionists are wrong about this as well.

These are just three of the hundreds of things that fish must have had in order to survive on land.

Furthermore, if fish did change into reptiles, then we should be able to find fossils of the millions

Evolutionists claim that creatures have evolved into each other by going through changes for millions of years. Some of them even say things such as that fish suddenly decided to go on land when they couldn't find enough food. Who knows? Maybe fish did not go on land to find food; maybe they went on land to watch television, just like the fish in the drawing. Isn't it just so illogical?

of transitional forms between fish and reptiles that ought to exist.

This means that there must have been many creatures with half legs, half lungs and half kidneys, and we ought to have been able to find their fossils today, but no such fossils exist.

The claim of evolutionists is so funny and so nonsensical, that it often becomes material for cartoons. As claimed by evolutionists, the ancestors of all living things—cats, snakes, plants, chicken and humans—were sea creatures. Even children would laugh at a person who claims such a thing!

ABOUT THE FISH CALLED THE COELACANTH

For years, evolutionists described a fish called the Coelacanth as a transitional form that almost made it ashore. In all their books and magazines they show this fish as their proof. They thought that the Coelacanth was extinct and no longer lived. This is why they made up a series of false stories when they examined the fossil of this fish.

Then, a fisherman caught a Coelacanth in his net. More people caught these fish many times. It became obvious that the Coelacanth is a normal fish. Furthermore, it wasn't preparing to come ashore, as evolutionists claim. Evolutionists were saying, "This fish lived in very shallow water, and so it was getting ready to go ashore". In reality, the Coelacanth lived in very deep water. It wasn't a transitional form as evolutionists claim. It was a true fish. Many more of evolutionists' false ideas have been exposed!

Evolutionists claim that the Coelacanth was a type of fish that was getting ready to go ashore. Then one day, a live Coelacanth was caught, and their mistakes were exposed.

107

NONSENSE!

Another false statement that evolutionists make is about how birds came about.

Their tall tale is that reptiles living on trees started to jump from tree to tree, and while they were jumping, they developed wings. Yet another tall tale is that some reptiles trying to catch flies were running flapping their forearms, and these forearms turned into wings.

Isn't it ludicrous to imagine a dinosaur developing wings while running? Things like this only happen in stories or in cartoons.

There is an even more important subject. These evolutionists say that this big dinosaur developed its wings when it was trying to catch flies. Well, then how did the fly take off? Where did the fly's wings come from? Instead of explaining how an enormous dinosaur started to fly, let them just explain how the little fly started to fly!

The reptile that the evolutionists claim is trying to fly.

You see, evolutionists can never explain this. As we explained earlier, the fly is one of the best flying creatures on earth. It can flap its wings 500 to 1000 times per second. As you know, it can manoeuvre with extreme ease. No matter how many stories evolutionists tell, they still cannot explain how a bird's wings came about. They don't even want to think about the wings of a fly!

The truth is that Allah created birds and flies with their wings and the ability to fly.

THE ARCHAEOPTERYX, WHICH EVOLUTIONISTS CALL A TRANSITIONAL FORM, IS IN FACT A COMPLETE BIRD!

Let us just present you a few of the differences between reptiles and birds.

1. Birds have wings, but reptiles don't.
2. Birds have feathers, but reptiles have scales.
3. Birds have a unique skeletal system and their bones are hollow. This makes them lighter and makes it easier for them to fly.

These are just a few differences that immediately come to mind. There are many more differences between these creatures.

If a species of reptile had turned into birds, there ought to have been many creatures that had lived in between the reptiles and the birds representing the phases of this change.

Fossil hunters should have been able to come

Birds could not have evolved from reptiles. They are both very different creatures. In this picture, you can see the difference between these two living classes.

across at least one of these fossils. That is, there must have been creatures with half wings, half feathered and half scaled bodies, half beaks and half mouths, and their fossils should have been found, but no such creature exists among the many fossils on earth. The fossils that are found belong either to a complete reptile or to a complete bird. This means that birds did not evolve from reptiles. Allah created birds just as He has created all other living things.

However, since evolutionists don't want to accept this, they try to convince people by inventing stories. How?

They have found the fossil of a bird called the Archaeopteryx and they have said that this bird is

It is totally impossible for reptile scales to turn into bird feathers. There is no resemblance between the two.

a transitional form between a dinosaur and a bird. They said, "The Archaeopteryx is the ancestor of all birds". To them, this is a creature that resembles a bird but is in fact a half dinosaur.

But this is false.

The Archaeopteryx is a complete bird!

Because:

1. The Archaeopteryx had feathers just like the birds of our time.

2. The Archaeopteryx had the same chest-bone, to which its wings were attached, as other flying birds.

3. The Archaeopteryx cannot be the ancestor of all birds, because fossils of birds that are more ancient than it have been found.

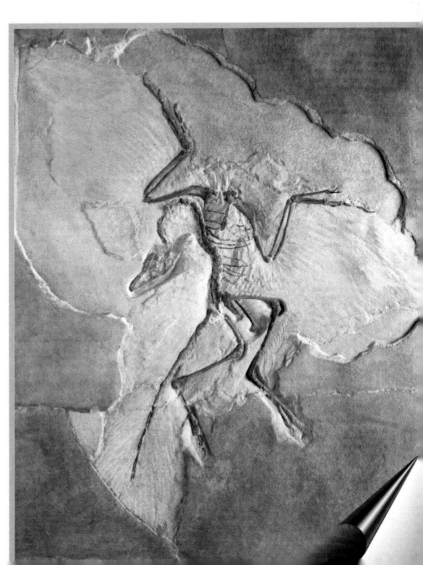

COULD A THING LIKE THIS EVER HAPPEN?

As you know, dolphins and whales are called sea mammals. These creatures, although they live in the sea, reproduce in the same way as do mammals on land. Fish, on the other hand, reproduce by laying eggs. Then how did sea mammals develop? Obviously, Allah has created them as well. Evolutionists, however, don't want to believe this. They cannot explain how dolphins and whales formed as well. Charles Darwin (the person who brought up the theory of evolution) had said, in his first book about the theory of evolution, something like this: Bears that went into the water to hunt fish all the time changed into whales. Yes, you read it right! He claimed that the hairy bears we know so well changed into metres and metres long whales after swimming in the sea a great deal.

Do you think it is possible for a bear to change into a whale, just because it swims a lot? Then shouldn't people who swim a lot change into sea mammals? Isn't it so funny?

These are fantasies that could only happen in stories. For example, in stories there are mermaids. Mermaids are half human and half fish. It could be that evolutionists are still under the influence of mermaid stories!

Darwin said that bears, while swimming in water, had changed into whales. Even some evolutionists do not believe this tall tale.

DO YOU BELIEVE A SWIMMING BEAR CAN TURN INTO A WHALE?

WELL, EVOLUTIONISTS DO!

THE TALE OF HUMAN EVOLUTION

The claims made by the theory of evolution are not limited only to these but they also declare that humans evolved from apes, and that thus apes are humans' ancestors.

Neither Darwin nor any other evolutionists have any proof to back up their claims. This statement is a totally fantasy. In reality, the reason for bringing forward a theory such as the theory of evolution is to make people forget that Allah created them. If people believe that they occurred by chance and their ancestor was an animal, then they feel no responsibility towards Allah. In turn, this causes them to forget all their religious values and become selfish. Selfish people lose such good feelings as love for their people and their families. You see, evolutionists try to distance people from such loyal feelings, and this is why they assert the theory of evolution. Their aim is to make people forget Allah, and for this reason they tell everyone, "Allah did not create you. You have come from apes, that is, you are an advanced animal."

In truth, Allah created humans. Compared to other living beings, the human being is the only creature that can speak, think, rejoice, and take decisions, is intelligent, can set up civilisations and can communicate at an advanced level. Allah is the One Who has given all these features to the humans.

Neither ape, nor any other creature for that matter, can talk, think or make decisions in the way we do.

EVOLUTIONISTS CANNOT SHOW ANY PROOF THAT HUMANS CAME FROM APES

Humans have always been humans and cats have always been cats.

In the field of science, it is very important to produce "proof". When you make a claim, and if you want others to believe it, then you have to show some proof. For example, if you introduce yourself to someone and say, "My name is Omar" and then this person says, "I do not believe that your name is Omar," then in that case you would have to have some proof that your name really is Omar. What could your proof be? An ID card could be a proof, or a birth certificate, or passport, or maybe your school report card, among other things. If you show one of these to that person, he will not object.

Now let us give a scientific example. There was a scientist called Newton who lived in the last century who claimed that there is something called the "gravity" on earth. He replied to those who asked him how he knew this, "When an apple falls off a tree, it falls on the ground. It doesn't stay in the air". That meant that there is a force pulling the apple to the ground and he called it "gravity".

Therefore, evolutionists have to show some proof to make their theories believable. For example, the theory of evolution states that the ancestors of humans are the apes. Then we should ask them: Where did you get this idea and where is your proof?

If the ancestors of humans are apes, we should find the fossils of creatures that are half human and half ape as confirmation. However, such a fossil has not been discovered until today. We have only found the fossils of humans or apes. This means that Evolutionists have absolutely no proof that apes are the ancestors of humans.

However, evolutionists try to trick people with their theories. How?

SOME TRICKS OF THE EVOLUTIONISTS:

1. Evolutionists show the fossils of extinct ape species as if they belong to creatures that are half human and half ape.

You probably have seen pictures such as the one above. You see, by drawing such pictures, evolutionists try to confuse people. In truth, such creatures have never existed. In the past, there used to be complete humans and complete apes, just like the ones today. None of the half ape and half human creatures shown in the above drawing has ever existed. This is far too unlikely to happen. As we stated earlier, not one fossil has been found to prove it.

However, evolutionists constantly try new tricks

on this topic. For example, while handling a fossil that belongs to an extinct species of apes, they claim it to be the fossil of a creature that was between apes and humans. As people are often not well informed about this topic, they are prone to believe the things that evolutionists say.

2. Evolutionists show the fossils of humans belonging to different races as if they are fossils of creatures that are half apes and half humans.

As you know, there are many different ethnic groups of people on earth. There are people belonging to different ethnic groups such as the Africans, Chinese, Red Indians, Turks, Europeans, Arabs and many others. Obviously, people belonging to different ethnic groups sometimes have different features. For example, the Chinese have eyes that are withdrawn to the back; some Africans have very dark skins and very curly hair. When you see a Red Indian or an Eskimo, you immediately know that they belong to a different ethnic group. You see, in the past, there were people of many other ethnic groups and some of their features were perhaps different from those of people today.

For example, the skulls of people belonging to the Neanderthal race were bigger than the skulls of people living today. Their muscles were a lot stronger than ours.

Evolutionists, however, used the differences between this race and ours as a way to deceive people. They say, for instance, when they find the

Just as it is impossible and nonsense for the change depicted in this drawing to have taken place, so are evolutionists' claims impossible and nonsense!

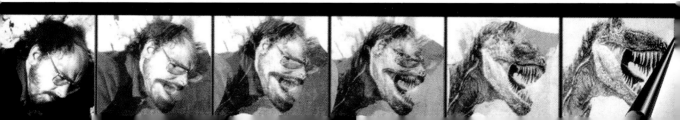

fossil of a Neanderthal skull, "This is the skull of humans' ancestors who have lived tens of thousands of years ago". Sometimes the skull fossils found were smaller than the average skull size of humans today. Holding a skull fossil, evolutionists say, "The owner of this skull was just at the point of changing from an ape into a human".

In reality, even today there are people

An Indonesian

A Chinese

A Greek

An Indian

An Aborigine

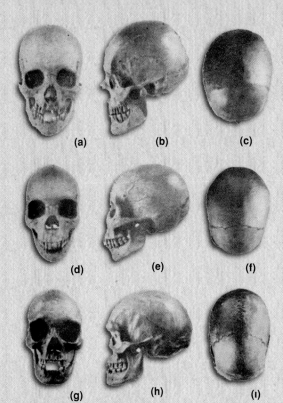
(a)　(b)　(c)
(d)　(e)　(f)
(g)　(h)　(i)

You can see above the different ethnic groups living on earth today. The skulls on the left also belong to different races. As you can see, many different races exist today, and most of these races have skulls that are very different from each other.

Evolutionists held these human skulls that are different from each other and presented them as if they are different species. In truth, the differences between the features of the skulls do not show different species but show different human races.

(a,b,c) Northern Races
(d,e,f) African Americans
(g,h,i) Australians

118

belonging to different ethnic groups that have smaller than average skulls. For example, the skull volume of Aborigines (Australian natives) is quite small, but this does not mean that they are half ape and half human. They are normal human beings just like you and all other human beings.

Consequently, we can see that the fossils evolutionists show as proof of humans evolving from apes either belong to earlier species of apes or human races that are now extinct. This means that half human and half ape creatures have never existed.

THE BIGGEST HOAXES OF EVOLUTIONISTS

1. The Piltdown Man Hoax

In 1912, the evolutionary scientists found a fossil of a jaw bone and a skull fragment. The jaw bone looked like that of an ape and the skull fragment looked like that of a human. According to the evolutionists, this creature was half human and half ape. These pieces were said to be about 500 thousand years old, and it was said they were proof that humans evolved from apes.

These bones were displayed as the proof of

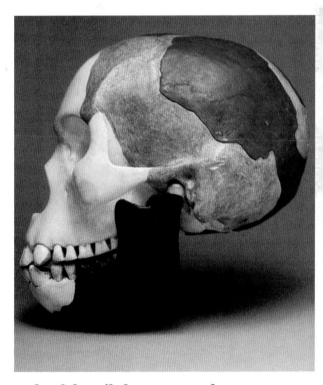

The fake Piltdown Man that evolutionists fabricated by fixing an ape's jaw to a human skull.

evolution for nearly 40 years, in various museums around the world. However, in 1949, some tests were applied to the bones and a very surprising result was attained: The jaw bone was not 500 thousand years old, but merely 2 or 3 years old. The skull bones belonged to the fossil of an ordinary human and they were only a couple of thousand years old.

The truth was realised later: Somebody had put an ape's jaw bone onto that of an ancient human skull, and covered it with some chemicals to make it look old.

When evolutionists could not find a half-human half-ape fossil, they attempted to manufacture a fake one.

This event was recorded in science history as the biggest hoax perpetrated by scientists.

The Nebraska Man drawn on the basis of a single tooth. It is extraordinary how imaginative evolutionists can be.

2. The Nebraska Man Hoax

In 1922, the fossil of a molar tooth was found. Evolutionists claimed that this tooth had the features of both humans and apes. Afterwards, a picture of a creature imagined to exist between man and the apes was drawn taking this single tooth as basis. Some evolutionists carried it even further and drew a family for this imaginary creature.

All these drawings were made taking a single tooth as a basis... Now think for a moment. If one of your teeth fell out, and someone who never met you before picks it up and claims

120

that he can draw an exact picture of you just by looking at that tooth, would you believe him? Wouldn't it sound just like a hoax, if he claimed that not only could he draw you but your family as well? Obviously, it is total nonsense to try to make a drawing of a creature and his family by only looking at a single tooth. In 1927, there was an amazing discovery. All the other skeletal pieces of the creature to which the tooth belonged were found. The tooth belonged neither to a human nor to an ape.

It belonged to a pig...

This event was a true disaster for evolutionists.

A drawing that appeared in the Sunday times on 5th April 1964

Maurice Wilson's Drawing

N. Parker's drawing from the National Geographic in September 1960

Do you see these drawings? Each evolutionist made different drawings while looking at the same skull. They seem uncertain as to how they should draw the creature. This is because such creatures have never existed. These are all fabrications of adult professors! What would your friends say if you found a bone while walking, made a drawing like these and said, "Let me show you drawings of creatures that lived long ago"?

You would probably never do such a thing, because you know that it wouldn't be intelligent. However, for some reason, evolutionary scientists cannot understand how stupid such a thing is.

THE PROOFS THAT PEOPLE DID NOT COME FROM APES:

1. Scientists have found fossils of humans that lived very long ago. These human fossils display no differences when compared to humans today. Moreover, the era during which these people lived is an era in which evolutionists claim that humans were still not formed. They claim that in that age, only the apes existed.

This 800 thousand-year-old skull belonged to a human being. It proves that evolutionists are fabricating hoaxes.

For instance, during the excavations of a cave in Spain, the fossils of a child who had lived about 800 thousand years ago were found. The face of this child had the same features as those of children today. However, if it was as evolutionists claim, there should have been no humans present 800 thousand years ago. There should have been half human half-ape creatures 800 thousand years ago. It was clear, when the fossil in Spain was found, that humans have existed as humans since they were first created. There have never been any half human and half ape creatures.

2. Scientists discovered the remains of a stone hut. When they calculated its age, they concluded that it was at least 1,5 million years old. This means that the humans who lived 1,5 million years ago were to some degree civilised. They were regular people just like the people of today. This makes total nonsense of

122

evolutionists' claims such as that humans evolved from apes, and that first there was primitive man (half human, half ape) who then evolved into today's mankind.

3. One of the oldest fossils found to date is that of the Turkana Boy, which is about 1.6 million years old. When the fossil was closely examined it was discovered that it belonged to a human about 12 years old, and that he would have been 1.80 m (5'90") tall if he had reached adulthood. This fossil alone, with its exact resemblance to human skeletons of today, was enough to destroy the belief that humans originated from apes.

4. Humans, among all living things, are the only creatures that can walk upright on two feet. Animals such as the horse, the dog and the ape are four-legged, and animals such as snakes, crocodiles and lizards are reptiles.

The theory of evolution claims that, millions of years ago, four-legged apes changed their walking style into a bent position. The apes continued to walk bent until their walk became upright. As a result, the human form was established. These claims made by the theory of evolution are not based on any scientific evidence but are rather based on total imagination. Studies made by scientists in recent years have proven that this claim of the

The Turkana Boy skeleton proves that the children were just like us even 1.6 million years ago.

It is impossible for apes that walk bent on four feet to change into human beings who walk upright on two feet.

evolutionists is totally unscientific nonsense!

Studies have shown that creatures best use their energies when they walk on either two feet or four. Creatures spend twice the energy when they try to walk bent and out of their natural posture.

Then, why would the apes walk bent, spending twice the energy, for thousands of years? It would be the same as if an adult human tried to crawl with a full load on his back. Would you, while able to walk comfortably on your two feet, suddenly decide to do a handstand and walk henceforth on your palms? Obviously, no creature would switch from a relaxed walking style to an uncomfortable walking style. Allah has created each creature with the ability to move in the most comfortable way.

In conclusion, the theory of evolution cannot answer the question, "Why did four-legged apes decide one day to walk on only two?"

THE BIGGEST DIFFERENCE

The biggest difference between an ape and a human is that humans have souls and apes don't. Humans have consciousness: they think, speak and convey their thoughts to others in rational sentences, make decisions, feel, develop tastes, know about art, paint, compose songs, sing and are full of love and values. All of these faculties are particular to the human soul. Animals do not have souls. No one other than a human could have these unique features.

Evolutionists are unable to answer this question. To resemble a human, an ape would have to go through many physical changes and would have to have the other faculties peculiar to human beings. Is there any force in nature that can give such abilities as painting, thinking, or composing to any ape? Of course not!

Allah created only humans with such abilities and He has not given animals any of these faculties. The human has been a human from the day he was created. The fish were always fish and the birds were always birds. No creature is the ancestor of another. Allah is the Creator of all humans and all other living beings.

Wouldn't it be unreasonable to say that humans originated from octopuses just because the eyes of an octopus look like that of a human?

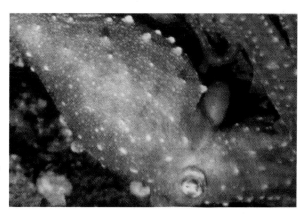

The reason that evolutionists claim that the humans have originated from apes is the physical resemblance between the two. However, other creatures on earth resemble humans more closely. For example, the parrots seen in the picture can talk. Octopuses have eyes just like those of a human. Cats and dogs listen to and follow orders, just like a person. What would you think if someone said that humans originated from dogs, parrots, or the octopus? You see, there is no difference between this idea and the stories evolutionists fabricate.

THE TOPICS THAT ARE SCARIEST FOR DARWIN AND EVOLUTIONISTS

As we mentioned at the beginning of our book, the eye is a very complex and perfectly designed organ. It is made up of 40 components, and it cannot function if even one of these components is missing.

All of these components have such intricate detail that it is impossible for them to have come about by chance. If just one of them, for example the lens, were missing, the eye could not function. Moreover, if just the lens and the pupil were to exchange positions, the eye could not function.

Even the tear that seems such a simple fluid is essential for the eye to function. An eye that does not produce tears will soon dry up and become blind. Furthermore, the tear's antiseptic properties protect the eye from germs.

The structure of an eye can be compared to that of a car. Many pieces make up a car. If all of its pieces were together but the gas pedal was missing, you would not be able to drive it. If one of the wires in its motor is cut, the car won't move. Eyes, just like a car, cannot function if even one piece is missing.

Evolutionists, however, are unable to explain how eyes formed, because it is impossible for even a single eye to happen by chance. Just think, is it probable that 40 different pieces come together at the same time and at the same place? This implies that pupil, lens, retina, eyelids, eye ducts, and others had to form by chance and join by themselves. This, of course, is impossible!

Darwin did not even want to think about the eye. It is impossible for the eye to happen by coincidence because the eye is perfect and yet so complex. It is the obvious truth that Allah has created the eye.

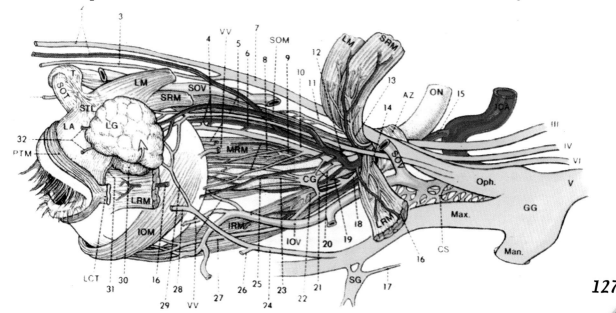

If you saw a car while you were out walking in the woods and asked how this car got there, and someone told you that some materials from the woods came together and formed this car, would you believe him?

If you saw a car while you were out walking in the woods and asked how this car got there, and someone told you that some materials from the woods came together and formed this car, would you believe him? Is a person in his right mind if he says that the motor, accelerator pedal, steering wheel, brakes, handbrake, windshield, chassis, and other pieces of a car happened to come into existence by chance and came together to form a vehicle?

The eye's structure is much more complicated and flawless than that of a car. Then we should wonder as well about the sanity of those who claim that the eye happened by chance.

Darwin was also not able to understand how the eye came about and he said, "I remember well the time when the thought of the eye made me cold all over." (Norman Macbeth, Darwin Retried: An Appeal to Reason, Boston; Gambit, 1971, page 101) The author of the theory was helpless when it came to explaining the perfect structure of the eye.

DARWIN ALSO DID NOT WANT TO THINK ABOUT THE FEATHERS OF THE PEACOCK...

Did you ever closely examine the feathers of a bird? The feathers of birds have very complex features that help them to fly. The feathers of each species of birds have different colours and we enjoy looking at them quite a lot. For example, the feathers of the peacock are so beautiful that people have made them the subjects of paintings or needlepoint canvases.

However, someone did not like the feathers of birds

at all, especially those of the peacock. That someone was Charles Darwin. This is because Darwin believed that the feathers of the peacock have happened by chance. However, these feathers are so breathtakingly beautiful that a person cannot believe that they have been formed by chance. Darwin said about these feathers, "Now, trifling particulars of structure often make me very uncomfortable. The sight of a feather in a peacock's tail, whenever I gaze at it, makes me sick!".

THE DATA BANK OF OUR BODY: DNA

Allah created the feathers of the peacock that we enjoy so much. Darwin, however, said that they "make him sick" since he did not want to believe this truth.

We have said before that there are trillions of cells in the human body. Each of these cells includes the data about all the person's features. What we have not yet mentioned is where inside the cell all of this data is stored.

Inside the nucleus of each cell, there are parts containing DNA. DNA holds all the information about the human body. All the data, such as the colour of your hair or your eyes, your inner organs, the way you look, your height, is all stored in your DNA. This data can be encoded using 4 different chemicals referred to by the letters, A, T, G, and C. Each letter shows the first letter of a

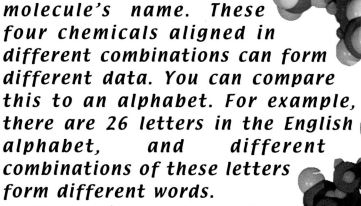

molecule's name. These four chemicals aligned in different combinations can form different data. You can compare this to an alphabet. For example, there are 26 letters in the English alphabet, and different combinations of these letters form different words.

There is a lot of information stored in the DNA. To realise just how vast this information is, we can make the following comparison: If we had to write down all the information in the DNA, we would end up with a large library of 900 volumes, each of 500 pages. This library would have to be about the length of a soccer field. However, all this knowledge has been fitted into a tiny molecule that we can't even see with our eyes.

So, who has put all this information in there? Who was able to fit it all in? Evolutionists have no choice but to continue their rehearsed line, "It all happened by chance".

This is a model of DNA. Inside DNA, there is enough data to fill about 900 volumes of an encyclopaedia.

However, it is very unlikely that something as difficult as this could happen by chance.

Above, we gave the example of a library. We said that the data in DNA is enough to pack volumes that would fill a library the length of a soccer field. When you see such a library, would you believe that the data in all those volumes was written as a result of a coincidence? Or rather, would you think that they were written by educated scholars and professors, and then published by a book company? Obviously, the latter is the logically correct answer.

Do you know what it sounds like

when evolutionists claim that DNA was formed by chance? It sounds like someone saying, "There was an explosion in the publishing house and all of these volumes of books happened by themselves."

Maybe while you were sitting at your desk in school, you came across a page that had the title "Geographic Features of the World", and when you asked who had written this page, a friend of yours replied: "A little while ago there was a bottle of ink on this paper. I incidentally spilled it and this writing appeared!" Would you not think that he had lost his mind?

Evolutionists claim something that is even more unlikely.

As even a page of writing cannot be without a writer, neither can a huge data bank such as DNA happen by itself.

Allah, Who is the Almighty and the All-wise, Who has power to do anything, Who is the Creator of the heavens and earth and whatever else in between them, is also the Creator of DNA.

ALLAH IS THE CREATOR OF ALL

Our Lord is the One Who has put billions of pieces of information in a place so small that our eyes cannot even see it.

Allah is the One Who has created us, our eyes, our hair, and our feet.

He is also the Creator of our families, parents, brothers and sisters, friends and teachers.

Allah is the One Who has created the food that we love for us, chocolates, cakes and candies, the fruits and vegetables that make us healthy and strong. If Allah had not created it, we would not have known what chocolate tasted like.

Allah has also given us the sense of taste and smell. If He had not given us these faculties, we would not have been able to taste the things that we eat. It would have been the same whether we ate a potato or a cake. Allah hasn't just created delicious and beautifully scented foods, He has also given us the faculties that will allow us to enjoy them.

You like some things, and you enjoy them and think of them as fun. It could be a dessert that you enjoy eating, a game that you enjoy playing, or an outing with people you love. You must never forget that Allah is the One Who makes it possible for you to enjoy such things.

Since Allah has great mercy for you, He always gives you pleasant and beautiful things.

To begin with, you did not exist. Just think, you

were nowhere before you were conceived. You were nothing. Allah created you. He made you out of nothing.

Then we must be grateful to Allah for each moment of our lives. In everything that we enjoy and love, we must remember Allah, and say, "O Allah I am forever grateful to you for all your offerings." If we come across a situation that we do not like, we should again pray to Allah, because He is the only One Who can put things right.

Allah always hears our prayers and responds to them, because He always knows what is in our thoughts. While reading this book, for instance, you are thinking of some things, but if you do not say them aloud, no one at home will know what you are thinking. Allah, however, knows your every thought and sees you all the time. Even when you think you are alone, Allah sees you and knows everything that you do.

For this reason, good people, even when they are by themselves, do not think, "Well no one can see me now" and then do wrong things. They know that Allah still sees and hears them even when no one else is around.

The drawing on the right is a cartoon of Darwin, the founder of the theory of evolution. This cartoon indicates that the theory of evolution has collapsed. The theory of evolution in our time has taken quite a beating just like Darwin in the cartoon.

CONCLUSION

The purpose of this book was to tell you that Allah is the Creator of the entire universe and all living things. It is obvious that Allah has created the whole universe. Some people, however, do not want to believe in the existence of Allah. This is why these people have brought forward tall tales such as the one called the theory of evolution.

While we talked about the existence of Allah in this book, we also explained the falsehood of the theory of evolution. We mentioned only a small number of the topics that prove the falsehood of the theory of evolution. To date, there has not even been one proof to justify the theory of evolution.

Now, you know that those who defend the theory of evolution are deceitful.

From now on, stop and think about everything you witness. If you see a mosquito, for instance, think about how it formed. Or while you are eating a fruit, think about the fact that Allah has given it its taste and smell. Don't ever forget when you look up at the sky and see the moon and the stars that Allah is the One Who put them there. Continue to think about Allah and continue to remind your friends about Allah. That is when Allah will truly love you and let you live a life full of beautiful blessings.

They said, 'Glory be to You! We have no knowledge except what You have taught us. You are the All-Knowing, the All-Wise.'
(Surat al-Baqara: 32)

ALSO BY HARUN YAHYA

Many people think that Darwin's Theory of Evolution is a proven fact. Contrary to this conventional wisdom, recent developments in science completely disprove the theory. The only reason Darwinism is still foisted on people by means of a worldwide propaganda campaign lies in the ideological aspects of the theory. All secular ideologies and philosophies try to provide a basis for themselves by relying on the theory of evolution.

This book clarifies the scientific collapse of the theory of evolution in a way that is detailed but easy to understand. It reveals the frauds and distortions committed by evolutionists to "prove" evolution. Finally it analyzes the powers and motives that strive to keep this theory alive and make people believe in it.

Anyone who wants to learn about the origin of living things, including mankind, needs to read this book.

238 PAGES WITH 166 PICTURES IN COLOUR

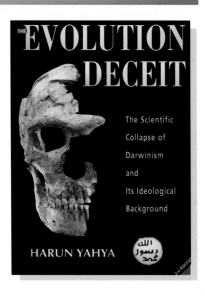

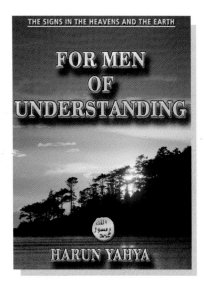

One of the purposes why the Qur'an was revealed is to summon people to think about creation and its works. When a person examines his own body or any other living thing in nature, the world or the whole universe, in it he sees a great design, art, plan and intelligence. All this is evidence proving Allah's being, unit, and eternal power.

For Men of Understanding was written to make the reader see and realise some of the evidence of creation in nature. Many living miracles are revealed in the book with hundreds of pictures and brief explanations.

288 PAGES WITH 467 PICTURES IN COLOUR

Darwin said: "If it could be demonstrated that any complex organ existed, which could not possibly have been formed by numerous, successive, slight modifications, my theory would absolutely break down." When you read this book, you will see that Darwin's theory has absolutely broken down, just as he feared it would.

208 PAGES WITH 302 PICTURES IN COLOUR

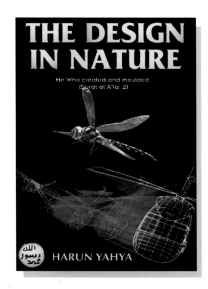

People who are oppressed, who are tortured to death, innocent babies, those who cannot afford even a loaf of bread, who must sleep in tents or even in streets in cold weather, those who are massacred just because they belong to a certain tribe, women, children, and old people who are expelled from their homes because of their religion... Eventually, there is only one solution to the injustice, chaos, terror, massacres, hunger, poverty, and oppression: the morals of the Qur'an.

<u>208 PAGES WITH 276 PICTURES IN COLOUR</u>

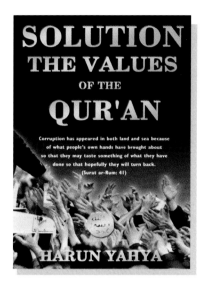

Have you ever thought that you were non-existent before you were born and suddenly appeared on Earth? Have you ever thought that the peel of a banana, melon, watermelon or an orange each serve as a quality package preserving the fruit's odour and taste?

Man is a being to which Allah has granted the faculty of thinking. Yet a majority of people fail to employ this faculty as they should... The purpose of this book is to summon people to think in the way they should and to guide them in their efforts to think.

<u>128 PAGES WITH 137 PICTURES IN COLOUR</u>

In the Qur'an, there is an explicit reference to the "second coming of the Jesus to the world" which is heralded in a hadith. The realisation of some information revealed in the Qur'an about Jesus can only be possible by Jesus' second coming...

<u>102 PAGES</u>

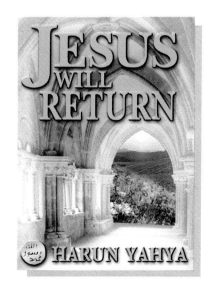

One of the major reasons why people feel a profound sense of attachment to life and cast religion aside is the assumption that life is eternal. Forgetting that death is likely to put an end to this life at any time, man simply believes that he can enjoy a perfect and happy life. Yet he evidently deceives himself. The world is a temporary place specially created by Allah to test man. That is why, it is inherently flawed and far from satisfying man's endless needs and desires. Each and every attraction existing in the world eventually wears out, becomes corrupt, decays and finally disappears. This is the never-changing reality of life.

This book explains this most important essence of life and leads man to ponder the real place to which he belongs, namely the Hereafter.

<u>224 PAGES WITH 144 PICTURES IN COLOUR</u>

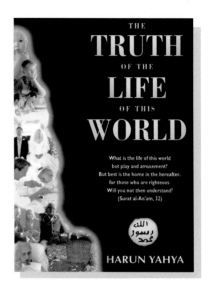

Colours, patterns, spots even lines of each living being existing in nature have a meaning. For some species, colours serve as a communication tool; for others, they are a warning against enemies. Whatever the case, these colours are essential for the well-being of living beings. An attentive eye would immediately recognise that not only the living beings, but also everything in nature are just as they should be. Furthermore, he would realise that everything is given to the service of man: the comforting blue colour of the sky, the colourful view of flowers, the bright green trees and meadows, the moon and stars illuminating the world in pitch darkness together with innumerable beauties surrounding man...

<u>160 PAGES WITH 215 PICTURES IN COLOUR</u>

Never plead ignorance of Allah's evident existence, that everything was created by Allah, that everything you own was given to you by Allah for your subsistence, that you will not stay so long in this world, of the reality of death, that the Qur'an is the Book of truth, that you will give account for your deeds, of the voice of your conscience that always invites you to righteousness, of the existence of the hereafter and the day of account, that hell is the eternal home of severe punishment, and of the reality of fate.

<u>112 PAGES WITH 74 PICTURES IN COLOUR</u>

Many societies that rebelled against the will of God or regarded His messengers as enemies were wiped off the face of the earth completely... Perished Nations examines these penalties as revealed in the verses of the Quran and in light of archaeological discoveries. This book is also available in German, French, Spanish, Russian and Portuguese.

<u>149 PAGES WITH 73 PICTURES IN COLOUR</u>

In a body that is made up of atoms, you breathe in air, eat food, and drink liquids that are all composed of atoms. Everything you see is nothing but the result of the collision of electrons of atoms with photons.

In this book, the implausibility of the spontaneous formation of an atom, the building-block of everything, living or non-living, is related and the flawless nature of Allah's creation is demonstrated.

<u>139 PAGES WITH 122 PICTURES IN COLOUR</u>

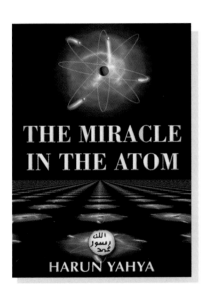

The evidence of Allah's creation is present everywhere in the universe. A person comes across many of these proofs in the course of his daily life; yet if he does not think deeply, he may wrongly å These aspects of ants create in one a great admiration for Allah's superior power and unmatched creation.

<u>165 PAGES WITH 104 PICTURES IN COLOUR</u>

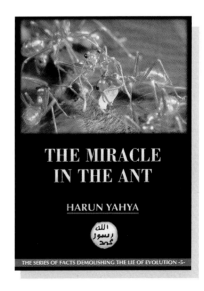

Dear children, while reading this book, you will see how Allah has created all the creatures in the most beautiful way and how every one of them show us His endless beauty, power and knowledge.

136 PAGES WITH 200 PICTURES IN COLOUR

Have you ever thought about the vast dimensions of the universe we live in? As you read this book, you will see that our universe and all the living things therein are created in the most perfect way by our Creator, Allah. You will learn that Allah created the sun, the moon, our world, in short, everything in the universe so that we may live in it in the most peaceful and happy way.

136 PAGES WITH 198 PICTURES IN COLOUR

MEDIA PRODUCTS BASED ON THE WORKS OF HARUN YAHYA

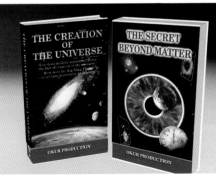

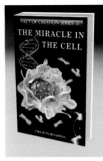

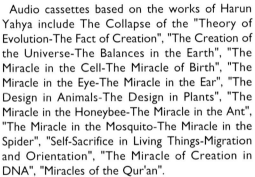

Audio cassettes based on the works of Harun Yahya include The Collapse of the "Theory of Evolution-The Fact of Creation", "The Creation of the Universe-The Balances in the Earth", "The Miracle in the Cell-The Miracle of Birth", "The Miracle in the Eye-The Miracle in the Ear", "The Design in Animals-The Design in Plants", "The Miracle in the Honeybee-The Miracle in the Ant", "The Miracle in the Mosquito-The Miracle in the Spider", "Self-Sacrifice in Living Things-Migration and Orientation", "The Miracle of Creation in DNA", "Miracles of the Qur'an".

HARUN YAHYA ON THE INTERNET

YOU CAN FIND ALL THE WORKS OF HARUN YAHYA ON THE INTERNET

• Scientific refutation of Darwinism, the greatest deception of our age.

• Dozens of books including hundreds of pages of information about the signs of God's creation.

• Extremely valuable works that will guide you to think on the real aspects of life by reading the morals of the Qur'an.

• Harun Yahya's political, scientific and faith-related articles that have appeared in various magazines and newspapers around the world.

• Audio recordings and documentary videos inspired by the works of Harun Yahya.

• And many more attractive presentations...

www.harunyahya.com
e-mail: info@harunyahya.com

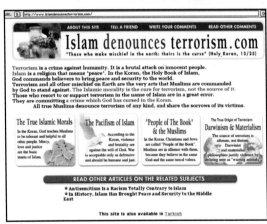

Islam is a religion that means "peace". In the Qur'an, the Holy Book of Islam, God commands believers to bring peace and security to the world. Terrorism and all other mischief on Earth are the very acts that Muslims are commanded by God to stand against. The Islamic morality is the cure for terrorism, not the source of it. This website is launched to reveal that any kind of terror and barbarism is against Islam, and Muslims share the sorrows of the victims of terrorism.

www.islamdenouncesterrorism.com
e-mail: info@islamdenouncesterrorism.com

Anti-semitism is a fanatical hatred felt for the Jewish people. This racist ideology has caused millions of Jews to be killed, persecuted, exiled and threatened. The religion of Islam aims to bring justice to the world. Just as it denounces all kinds of racism, so it denounces anti-semitism. Muslims criticize Zionism, but defend the right of Jews to live in peace and security.

www.islamdenouncesantisemitism.com
e-mail: info@islamdenouncesantisemitism.com

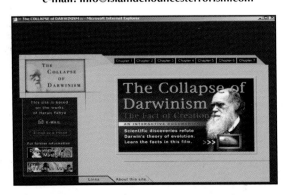

This site is part of a chain of sites set up parallel to Harun Yahya's official homepage (www.harunyahya.org) This work is intended to inform the whole world of some important truths, not for commercial ends. The most important of these truths is the fact of creation: Life and man did not emerge by themselves, as the result of chance, as materialist philosophy claims. In the same way that God created the universe from nothing, He also created and gave shape to living things and man. This is a fact backed up by contemporary scientific discoveries. In this site is a documentary that genuinely explains the truth of creation.

www.evolutiondocumentary.com
e-mail: info@evolutiondocumentary.com